Remember Yo

Erik G. LeMoullec, D.C.

Erik G. LeMoullec

Remember Your Name

Dedication

In loving memory of my Baba and Saba, who knew the book was being written but never saw it completed. Our family knows your story. Now the world can.

Disclaimer

This is a work of narrative nonfiction. The author has tried to recreate events, locales and conversations from his grandfather's memories of them. In order to maintain their anonymity, in some instances he may have changed the names of individuals and places, he may have changed some identifying characteristics and details such as physical properties, occupations and places of residence.

Contents

1: The Long Ride Home

The rifle blast behind Teddy signaled the ending of a Jew's life. The spray of blood on the back of his neck confirmed who it was: Jacob – a boy not more than sixteen years old. The warmth of the red life-containing substance immediately cooled in the sub-zero weather, sending chills down Teddy's malnourished spine. They had been marching for days towards Tirol under unbearable conditions, their numbers dwindling every hour. Jacob was just another casualty.

Teddy, now fifteen, had witnessed more suffering in his short life than he cared to remember. He'd watched as his beautiful hometown of Lodz was transformed into an overcrowded, underfed ghetto. He'd viewed the decline of humanity as neighbors stole from one another and ratted each other out to the gestapo for mere scraps of food. He'd accepted the fact that he would never see his family again as they were selected for deportation out of the ghetto. Where they went nobody knew, but the rumors were not promising. He'd ridden on a cattle car train stuffed to the brim with Jews, suffering days of standing in piles of human waste only to arrive at hell's doorstep. He'd survived another selection which, he later learned, had sent those unlucky enough to be chosen straight to their deaths. Now, here he was contemplating his luck on a frigid march to a town he had never heard of.

A hollow clunk of Teddy's wooden clog on a rock broke the silence after the gunshot. Pain echoed through his entire frostbitten body but he knew better than to cry out. The last thing he wanted was added attention from the SS. He stumbled forward, catching himself on Kwart's back, stopping him from falling into the snow.

Kwart, a stranger to him four years ago, was all Teddy had to hold onto. He'd vowed to look after him after Teddy's family had been deported from the ghetto. So far, he was doing a good job. Teddy was still alive.

Kwart asked if he was okay. Teddy nodded. He shook off the stabbing pain and continued marching. It was his only option. Another crack of a rifle a few meters back ended another Jew's misery. Teddy put his head down and pressed on, contemplating when it would be his turn. *Why is this happening?* he wondered.

The snow picked up, making an already impossible march impassable. A commotion up ahead commanded Teddy's attention and he looked up to see what it was. Shlomo had given up. Refusing to go on, he took off his ragged striped prison shirt and handed it to the man behind him. Shevah Goren, the man to his right, was lucky enough to get his wooden clogs, which appeared to be in relatively good condition. Shlomo stood still and stared up into the night sky waiting for death to greet him.

Each man that passed by tapped Shlomo's shoulder with his own emaciated hand, a silent goodbye: *I will see you soon*. It was Teddy's turn. He tapped Shlomo's bony shoulder and stepped forward before feeling a weak hand grab him and pull back. Teddy turned to see Shlomo tug out his final piece of stale bread from his trouser pocket and hand it to him. A gift of the highest degree. They locked eyes and nodded before Teddy turned to march on.

Shlomo had given life to Teddy's family's business back in Lodz. He had been one of their first customers and a great referrer of business. Now he attempted to extend Teddy's own life. Eight steps later another rifle shot sounded. Too afraid to turn and look, Teddy could only assume who it was.

He trudged through the snow, trying to distance himself from the feelings of death behind him and pondered on his family. Where were they? Were they still alive? Would he ever see them again? Then a morbid feeling overtook him. Would he live to see his sixteenth birthday? Would he ever get the chance to have a family of his own?

#

Sixty-nine years later and four thousand miles away, a very different journey was taking place from Woodbury, Connecticut, to Rockland County, New York, on a rainy Saturday morning. My wife, Shannon, our fourteen-year-old daughter, Hayden, and I were on our way to Pomona, twenty-five miles north of New York City, where my grandparents lived. The average drive was between an hour and a half to an hour and forty-five minutes. Today, for any number of reasons, we had been in the car for two hours already and were not even close to the Tappan Zee Bridge.

Shannon knew the commute well. She drove from Woodbury to Ardsley in Westchester County, NY, almost every day for work. As a managing quality compliance auditor, she travelled to different vendors her company used, to perform audits. She was no stranger to the car. Her typical commute was an hour and fifteen minutes without traffic but that never happened. Traffic was inevitable. Her drive was realistically an hour and thirty to an hour and forty-five minutes each way. I could feel her peering over at me as I was busy driving.

"Welcome to my world."

"Yeah, yeah, yeah," I responded. My knuckles whitened as I tightened my grip on the steering wheel. "I don't understand why we're not moving."

"Most of the time there isn't any reason at all; people just don't know how to drive," shrugged Shannon, sounding as though she'd asked herself the same question a million times. "Drive carefully."

Shannon and I are opposites when it comes to driving. Shannon comes home late from work, having endured miles of traffic. I'm a chiropractor in Woodbury and commute five minutes up the road. My only complaint is that I don't get to listen to enough Howard Stern on the car radio, which, of course, I would never say aloud.

In everyday life our personalities are the opposite of how they are in the car. The auditor in Shannon makes her detailed, organized and to the point in everything she does. If a problem arises, she pulls out a categorized plan of how to fix it. I, on the other hand, have a laid-back, go-with-the-flow attitude.

Coffee House was streaming on SiriusXM satellite radio. I play this channel at my office too and enjoy the acoustic renditions of famous songs. Occasionally, a well-known musician will play their version of someone else's song giving it a neat twist. Currently on was an Elton John classic, 'Rocket Man'.

The rain picked up outside. Each drop pounded the roof in rhythm with the song, adding an interesting bass component to an already fantastic tune. The wind grew more powerful, making tree branches dance to a song never heard before.

"Are we almost there?" sighed Hayden, who was sitting behind Shannon.

"Almost," I answered, not needing another reminder of the time.

"How much longer, do you think?" she persisted.

"About fifteen minutes once we cross over the bridge," Shannon chimed in.

"Will there be traffic after the bridge?" Hayden continued.

"God, I hope not," I answered.

The 2008 Jeep Liberty was at a complete stop with no signs of movement ahead. Time slowed. Twenty seconds felt like five minutes.

"Get over!" shouted Shannon at the first sight of the left lane moving. Her traffic experience was taking over. Before I could react, the gap closed.

"I will next time," I answered.

"I guess I'm the true Znamirowski in the car," Shannon boasted sarcastically.

Znamirowski was my mother's maiden name. The running joke in the family was that a person was only considered a Znamirowski if they had balls. My mom, Eti, always joked that I met and married the perfect woman because she had balls. Shannon had no fear about asking anybody anything or taking risks. She always made sure she got her way. She became an honorary Znamirowski by marriage. The joke, of course, was my getting the short end of the stick in the Znamirowski department. I obviously had "tiny balls" because I was shy, soft-spoken and content, making the best with what life had given me. Being Znamirowski became synonymous with winning and doing whatever was needed to become successful and, essentially, survive.

Hayden was always an inquisitive girl. From a young age in daycare, she was the first to notice the sign language the teachers taught to the children too young to communicate with words. Simple commands – more, eat, hot, done, please and thank you – came easily to her. Then, as soon as she was able to speak, she took full advantage of language and had not stopped since. She was a beautiful girl with an even mix of characteristics from her parents.

Her relaxed personality, light brown hair, high cheekbones, round nose and heartwarming smile are mine. The hazel/green eyes, wavy hair, cute pointed chin, infectious laugh and inquisitiveness come from Shannon.

"Do you know what today is?" I asked Hayden.

"Saturday," she responded, half paying attention, half staring at the rain.

"Well yes, but besides that," I continued.

"Saba's birthday," Hayden answered, rolling her eyes to show she had no interest in taking part in the conversation.

"That's right. Do you know how old he is?" I pressed.

Seeing no way to ignore her father, Hayden punched pause on her iPod and let out an angry sigh. "Ninety," she guessed, her voice lacking excitement.

"No, not ninety, a little lower," Shannon jumped in.

"Mom, not you too," Hayden returned. "He's eighty."

"Higher," prompted Shannon.

"Really?" asked Hayden, getting more frustrated with each question. "Is he eighty-five?"

"What's eighty-five minus one?" I continued prompting.

"Eighty-four," Hayden declared, glad the guessing game was finished. She reached down and turned her iPod back on.

An acoustic 'You and I Both' by Jason Mraz came on the car radio. I sang aloud to the song, bobbing my head, pretending I was good enough to be on *American Idol*. I would more realistically get onto the outtakes than the top ten but I didn't care: I was with my family. Hayden laughed at my attempted high notes, which she could hear over her iPod, while Shannon jokingly clawed at the window, shouting, "Stop!"

"Hey, Dad?" Hayden asked.

"Yes, cutie," I responded.

"Why does Saba talk like that?"

A bolt of lightning flashed in front of the car, as if it were the perfect punctuation to Hayden's question. My pupils dilated at its brightness and clarity. At that moment, time stood still. Jason Mraz and the radio ceased to exist. There was no traffic and even the rain froze, as if God himself had pushed the pause button. To anyone else in the world that would be a simple question to answer. But I did not hear a question: it was a line echoing in my past. A question I myself asked many years ago as a child. The words reverberated in my head, sending me spiraling down to moments of my life I had not thought about in years. The memories were not about Saba's accent but of time I'd spent with him.

Saba and I were inseparable when I was a child. This was in part because both my parents worked during the day so they dropped me off at my grandparents' house after preschool, but we also enjoyed each other's company. Saba often said I reminded him of himself as a child. We were a team.

From a young age, I always watched Saba work. He was a carpenter, a Jack-of-all-trades and great at every one of them. He never spoke much but was always thinking. Willing to try learning new things, he acquired skills quickly. I looked up to Saba, seeing how people were grateful to him for the work he did, and Saba lived through me, replacing his lost youth. He made sure all his grandchildren had the childhood he was not able to have.

I tried to formulate a response for my inquisitive daughter but my mind would not let me. It took me to a place I had not thought about in years, wrapping me up in a flashback.

I remembered lying on the floor with Saba as we repaired a wall-mounted air conditioner in the apartment complex my grandparents ran. Of course, I could not do any mechanical work but I held flashlights and grabbed any tool Saba needed. We wore oversized sunglasses bought on a trip to Disney World the previous year. I constantly moved the flashlight to stop the shades from falling off and Saba could not see what he was doing. We laughed the whole time. I was almost four.

Images of getting permission from my mom to climb the roof of a house Saba was building entered my mind. I remembered sitting next to him, watching intently as he put shingles into place. My father, Bob, held on to me making sure I would not lose my footing on the steep roof.

I tried making the thoughts stop but they continued playing. I remembered helping Saba remove copper piping from a damp, moldy basement when I was nine. My cousin, Seth, and I were terrified when a large, hairy, brown spider hung down near the basement exit. We panicked but Saba walked over to save the day. He hit it with a hammer, only to find the body was rubber and the hair was mold.

I'm the oldest grandchild. My grandmother, Baba, is from Odessa, Russia. My grandfather, Saba, is from Lodz, Poland. After the war, they met in Israel and had two girls: my mother, Eti, and my Aunt Tova. They immigrated to America in the early 1960s. Being first-born generation in a country breathing hope and prosperity was a fantasy for Holocaust survivors. Their grandchildren now stood in the face of everything that was meant to cut them down over fifty years ago.

Then it hit me. The chaotic flow of memories melded into one solid scene. I was fifteen years old. I was helping Saba pour cement in Aunt Tova and Uncle Michael's back yard for a hot tub base. I shoveled it onto the platform, failing miserably. Cement was everywhere. Saba watched me struggle for a few minutes then calmly walked over, placed a hand on my shoulder and said, "*My shayne boitchikle*, I can do." I looked up, nodding in approval, and took a few steps back. I watched Saba flawlessly shovel the remaining cement onto the platform.

Minutes of casual conversation went by regarding the *chulnt* that Baba was preparing for dinner. We joked about Baba not sleeping next to Saba after eating *chulnt* because of the awful gas the potato and barley stew gave him. We laughed, and then I brought up a random question.

"Saba, why do you talk like that?"

An honest question from an innocent boy required more than the simple answer of an accent from being born in another country. Saba, caught off guard, stopped leveling cement, turned around and looked in my eyes.

"Growing up wasn't easy for your Saba, Erikle," he started.

"Yeah, I have hard tests myself," I joked.

Saba chuckled. "It was different for me," he continued. "The world was different."

The afternoon conversation between grandfather and grandson ingrained itself in my mind. Sure, I knew of the Holocaust – Saba went through it – but I never knew its exact meaning.

Saba's life story encompassed enough information to fill twenty lifetimes. I learned the delicate balance between life and death, and their overlapping. How a simple wave of a hand in one direction meant life, in the other, death. Endless painful feelings of hunger and the tricks it played on a person's mind. Food's importance taking on a completely new meaning. Being surrounded by people but feeling entirely alone. Seeing death every day. The endless smell of burning bodies and hair linked with inevitable feelings of one day ending up like that.

Then the good shone through. Saba spoke about life, and the people who made it possible for him to keep his. Kwart, who saved him many times. Partisans of Bricha, bringing purpose to his existence. Secret stashes of food supplied by the butcher and Helena in the munitions factory at Görlitz. His father Simcha, his mother Touba, his two sisters Pola and Esther, his Aunt Rose and cousin Cila, and his two friends, Chaim and Asher. Without their help, Saba would have died. Their deeds had not been in vain. Remembering them encouraged him to press on.

None of this meant anything to me yet, at least not in any meaningful way. I later came to appreciate them whenever Saba put down a pail of mortar during work or his fork at a family meal and revealed stories of a time long past.

Honking from the '95 red Pontiac Grand Am snapped me into the present. The Ford Explorer in front of it had moved up a whole five feet. Jason Mraz was still on Coffee House. Rain continued to fall in thick blanketing sheets, drenching everything in the May shower.

I did a double check on myself, needing reassurance that everything tumbling through my mind was memory. I breathed deeply, slowing my heart rate, then fixed my seatbelt because suddenly it felt too tight for comfort. Still clutching the steering wheel, cutting off circulation, I loosened my grip and looked into the rear view mirror, but, to my surprise, Hayden was not the person looking back.

I looked away, blinking hard. *What's going on*? I wondered. Glancing back at the mirror, Hayden still was not there. I knew this person, but the fact I was staring at him was impossible. I looked straight ahead, eased off the brake and allowed the jeep forward, and then peered back at the mirror.

The person staring back was me as a fifteen year old. It was as if my quick journey down memory lane had forgotten to take the younger version of myself, back. *Can this really be happening*? I wondered. Perplexed, I turned to see who was sitting there. Hayden looked back, awaiting my answer. I faced forward again, looking once more into the mirror. Just as before, teenage Erik was there. His dark brown, innocent eyes turned sincere as we made eye contact. He nodded his head in approval and it became clear to me.

Young Erik's hair lengthened and lightened. His eyes changed to hazel green as his features became more feminine, slowly morphing back into Hayden, the person who was rightfully sitting there. I knew what I was supposed to do. I cleared my throat, looked at my beautiful daughter in the mirror and answered her question:

"Growing up wasn't easy for your Saba, Hayden."

#

2: A Child's Innocence

Springtime in Lodz, 1938, for a nine-year-old boy was like springtime any other year. Teddy, born at the end of May 1929, could care less about the major changes happening in Poland's political climate as long as the weather warmed. Winters in Lodz were bitterly cold, forcing children to play indoors.

Teddy's real name was Tanek, but everyone called him by his Hebrew name, Tanchum. His parents named him after Tanchum Minski, his maternal grandfather, who'd died before he was born. Tanchum Senior had been a cantor in the Stara synagogue, the oldest in Lodz, located at 20 Wolborska Street. A well-respected man in town, his kindness towards others that emerged through stories about him earned Teddy's respect and admiration early on.

Lodz's economy boomed before the war. The city was known as the second Manchester or the "Polish Manchester" because of its production of textiles. Amid high volumes of factories, it also had a successful tailoring industry. Wherever a person was in the city, they could always hear the hum of the mills and referred to them as sounds of hope and prosperity. Teddy joked with his father about one day being richer than Izrael Kalmanowicz Poznanski, who was the textile magnate and philanthropist responsible for all the factories in Lodz.

If a person was not attending school, they worked. Artisans, newspaper delivery boys, shoemakers, lawyers, doctors and pretzel sales representatives all worked under the omnipresent hum of factories. Trolley cars ran constantly, taking passengers to their destinations. Lodz had the hustle and bustle of a flourishing industrial city.

The Jewish section, in the mid to northern part of Lodz, was a city within a city, rich in community and culture. The Jewish Community Counsel organized and maintained a Mikva, kosher slaughterhouse, and an education system for the poor, having established a diversified educational network. A number of Yeshivas opened, along with a Jewish school for girls. It had theatres for movies, plays, concerts and a thriving nightlife.

Teddy's parents always told him to stick to the Jewish section when venturing about. Virtually no hate existed in the Jewish Quarter but problems arose if one went outside its perimeter.

Teddy lived on the fourth floor of a four-story apartment building on Mielczarskiego Street, located in a beautiful section of Lodz. Handsome rows of trees bloomed in spring, lining both sides of the cobblestone street. On the first floor was an ice cream shop. The owner, a grumpy old man, always had remnants of ice cream in his beard. He yelled at children frequently for hanging out in front of his store, telling them they were bad for business, which never made sense, considering they represented sixty percent of it.

From his bedroom window, he easily saw over the two-story building across the way onto a small field. There, he met up with friends before walking to school or planning activities.

Throughout childhood, Teddy and his friends had a knack for finding trouble, but getting out of it required finesse. Teddy's ability to get out of tight scrapes came naturally to him. He learnt early on to react quickly and think on his feet. He had an innate ability to make a buck, which became useful later on.

The Znamirowski family lived in a spacious three-bedroom apartment. Mielczarskiego Street, considered a posh part of town, had easy access to a wide assortment of shops. There were nineteen other apartments in their building, all containing families with children.

The number of children living in close proximity was paradise. The field across the street only bettered the situation. No matter the time of year, there was always the field. It adapted, allowing for seasonal games of tag and soccer in summer, snowball fights and snowmen in winter.

The biggest luxuries were running water and electricity. Most of Teddy's friends lived in other complexes having one or the other. Some had neither. When the Znamirowski children came home from school, wonderful smells wafted from the kitchen, welcoming them. Fresh *perogies*, stuffed with variations of meats, potatoes and cheeses, and smothered with onions would fry on the stove. The occasional *babka* or *mizeria*, a little more on the healthy side, was a welcome treat. Friends routinely stopped by to say "hello" on their way home, sneaking a few delicious snacks.

Even with the apartment's ample space, Teddy's two sisters, Pola who was twelve, and Esther who was four, had to share a bedroom. They were jealous that Teddy – the middle child – got his own room: being the only boy had its benefits.

Despite their differences, the three children were very close. They walked around the city together and looked after each other. They took care of one another, always putting family first.

Pola gave the impression that she had the world figured out, yet she still clung to her parents at the first sign of trouble. She had her mother's height, already over five feet tall, and her father's features of dark brown wavy hair and blue eyes. Being the oldest child, she took it personally to watch out for Teddy and Esther. She made sure their clothes were presentable and they washed up before supper. She also tried her hardest to keep Teddy out of trouble, which became increasingly harder to do.

Esther, on the other hand, was the total opposite of Teddy. She was easy to take care of, listened to directions and wanted to be like both her mother and Pola. Pola taught her how to be well-mannered and spent time combing her hair and applying makeup. Esther was a twin – her sibling had died shortly after birth. She resembled both Teddy and their mother with lighter features, dirty blonde-red hair and blue eyes. Still too young to go to school, she stayed home with her mother who educated her in *alef-beits* and a few songs so she would be ahead of her class when she was old enough to attend.

Teddy and Pola went to public school. They were lucky in the sense that school was only a few blocks away. Their friends whined about long walks and the complaining doubled when the weather turned worse.

 Pola enjoyed school. She looked at it as a way to learn about the world. Teddy preferred playing outside or helping his father in the shop. It was not that he did not like school, it just was not enough of a challenge for him. People called him a *"yiddisher kop"*.

He was particularly fast at picking up languages from other countries. At nine he was fluent in Yiddish, Polish, German and Russian. The amazing part was how he spoke them without any accent. Neighbors who knew those languages were stunned, swearing he must have immigrated to Poland from the country whose language he spoke.

The children hardly missed a day of school. Days to lie in bed and recover did not exist in the Znamirowski household. If the children were ill enough to miss school, they read short stories and followed up with presentations of the book to their parents. Going to school always seemed the better option.

Their father occasionally sent Teddy to pick up supplies for his shop. He calculated how much the trolley car and supplies would be and gave Teddy the exact change, but Teddy had other plans in mind. He often skipped the trolley altogether and ran or rode his bike to the store for supplies, pocketing the remaining *groshy* for himself. He considered it his payment for delivery.

Sporadically, on the walk home from school, Teddy stopped by the local street corner kiosk two blocks from his apartment and bought a new *Tarzan* magazine with the *groshy* he saved. Stories of Tarzan made Teddy's imagination run wild. He pretended to be in the jungle, running up and down streets screaming. Movie theatres were also a luxury Teddy frequented with his friends. Theatre was the way Teddy watched his imagination come to life.

The sun shone uninhibited one Saturday morning at the end of June. Teddy and Pola had finished their chores for the morning when a tapping at Teddy's bedroom window caught their attention. They turned to face each other, confused. They heard a second tap, then a third. Teddy walked to the window to see what was happening. As he lifted it open, a pebble missed his face by centimeters. Unfortunately, Pola was not so lucky. The pebble hit her square in the right cheek, knocking her down to the floor.

"*Drek*," exclaimed Pola, lifting herself up.

She barged to the window to see who had thrown the stone.

"Tanchum, *lets geyn!*" Chaim exclaimed.

Chaim had been Teddy's best friend since age two, and was the reason he got into trouble so often.

"Tanchum, *kumen gikh.*" He wanted his friend to hurry up.

Pola grabbed Teddy and pushed him out of the way. Luckily, he landed on the bed. She screamed down to Chaim, "Why can't you knock on the door like a normal person?"

"Sorry, Pola," Chaim responded, semi-sarcastically.

"You hit me in the cheek," she returned.

"I was aiming for Tanchum!" said Chaim.

"Well, you have horrible aim, you *schmendrick!*" Pola answered.

They both laughed.

A minute later, like a stampede of wildebeest, Chaim ran upstairs into the apartment, heading for Teddy's room. By the time he got there, Teddy had finished tying his shoelaces.

"Let's go, Tanchum. It's a beautiful day for trouble!" Chaim exclaimed.

"I'm hurrying!" answered Teddy.

Before Teddy could warn Chaim, Pola snuck up and punched him in the shoulder. More out of surprise than pain, Chaim let out a yelp and turned around. Pola held a piece of meat up to her right cheek, applying gentle pressure to stop the swelling from where the stone had hit.

"If this bruises, I'm going to hurt you," she promised.

"It could only make you look better!" answered Chaim.

Pola stuck her tongue out at him, following it up with another punch.

Once outside, Teddy saw Chaim was not exaggerating. It was a beautiful day. The sky was an incredible shade of blue with no clouds in sight. The rows of trees on either side of the street were a lush green, except for the one weeping willow whose long flowing branches had a soft hint of yellow.

Pola brought Esther out to enjoy the day. Her cheek was a soft rosy color with no swelling. Esther kept herself occupied on the sidewalk with blocks and an old handmade doll handed down to her from Pola, who'd received it from their mother, who in turn had got it from their grandmother. The doll showed its age, littered with scars from tears sewn back together. Its name was Anka and it was a security blanket for Esther. It was becoming harder to separate the two. Trying to get Esther out the door without Anka only worked occasionally.

Pola was also on the sidewalk, rotating between her yoyo and jump rope. Jumping rope was her favorite things to do. The highest number she'd ever jumped without stopping was one hundred and twenty-four. She made it her mission to beat it before summer ended. The yoyo was a newer toy and she could not get the hang of it. Teddy teased her often because he did it without difficulty.

Teddy and Chaim ran down the street, chasing after a bicycle tire with a makeshift aluminum tube Teddy had created. Whoever kept the tire rolling the longest was the winner. Being fast on his feet, Teddy won constantly. Looking towards the sky, he batted his hands on his chest screaming out like Tarzan. Chaim, a little heavier, had trouble keeping up.

Pola decided she'd had enough playing outside and took Esther upstairs to the apartment. Teddy and Chaim continued running around when the sweet smell of ice cream overwhelmed them. The growling in their stomachs became hard to ignore. Simultaneously, the boys reached into their pants for money and put their heads down in defeat. Their pockets were empty. Teddy knew asking his parents for money would result in a no and an explanation why he did not need ice cream, but he was determined. He looked at Chaim.

"Follow me," he said.

They headed towards the ice cream shop. Every step closer made them salivate more. The smells in front of them made the hair on the back of their necks stand up. Their eyes widened. One could not help but smile at the joys the shop had to offer.

As Teddy reached out to open the door, the fragrance hit him hard. All the flavors – cacao, coffee, vanilla, lemon and wild strawberry – combined into one fantastic smell of sweet deliciousness.

Three steps into the shop, Teddy looked down to his left and started screaming, "Mouse, mouse, mouse!"

Chaim, confused at first at not seeing any mouse, quickly grasped what Teddy was up to. He followed his lead, screaming and jumping to get out of the way. The scene unfolding frazzled the grumpy storeowner. He leapt to attention, bits of ice cream falling from his beard, and ran to see what the commotion was. When he reached the boys, Teddy pointed, screaming, "It went over there!"

"What are you talking about, I see no mouse," frowned the old man.

"It was there, I saw it," Teddy proclaimed. "It was grey with a long tail and black eyes."

"You didn't see any mouse," the owner responded.

"I'm telling you, I did" Teddy answered, forcing himself to keep a straight face. "Look, there are pieces of *drek* everywhere!"

"I see no such thing," said the old man, his voice riddled with anger. "I'm going to give you both a shellacking you'll never forget!"

He reached for his leather belt, and started unbuckling it. Chaim's expression turned fearful, seeing the strap, but Teddy stood firm, not allowing the situation to overwhelm him.

Keeping calm, Teddy explained, "I'm going to notify the building about this mouse."

"There is no mouse!" the owner screamed at the top of his lungs.

"Says you," Teddy answered. "But you would say that, not wanting anyone to know you have mice here."

"What?" the man asked, flustered.

"Mice in your shop can't be good for business and it's not good for the building either. I need to report this," Teddy replied.

"No! You can't!" the old man cried. "Here, I'll give you both ice creams if you keep quiet and get out of my shop."

"You've got a deal!" said Teddy, allowing the smile to take over his face.

The boys walked out of the shop, Teddy with vanilla and Chaim with wild strawberry ice cream. Teddy thought it best to enjoy their treats out of sight. They headed over to the field across from Teddy's apartment, laughing at the incident.

"Did you see his face?" Chaim chuckled.

"I can't believe that worked!" said Teddy. "This ice cream is delicious!"

Finishing their ice creams, the boys parted ways for the night.

A voice greeted Teddy when he opened his apartment's front door.

"Tanchum, come here."

He could tell by his father's voice's tone that whatever was going to happen next was not good. Teddy cautiously walked to the dining room where his father and mother waited.

"Sit down," said Simcha.

Before Teddy felt the cushioned chair beneath him, Touba asked, "Would you like to explain what happened today?"

Teddy knew what she meant. Word spread fast on Mielczarskiego Street. It travelled sooner than intended with the ice cream shop on the first floor of this same building.

Teddy looked up at his parents, finding it hard to keep eye contact. He was an honest child and could not lie to anyone, especially his family. He explained the entire situation: the incredible smell, not wanting to ask his parents for money, the fact the idea was entirely his. Looking up, he saw Pola and Esther peeking around the kitchen corner. Pola strained hard not to laugh. Her cheeks were a brighter shade of red than earlier that morning.

Simcha asked, "But why would you do that, Tanchum?"

Teddy told them everything. Every day the grumpy storeowner yelled. He told children never to play in front of his shop and he could not stand them. The man never appreciated people coming into the shop and acted as though it was a chore rather than a privilege to serve the delicious treat. When Teddy had gone into the ice cream shop, he'd felt compelled to do something nasty because the old man was not a nice person.

"Not all people are nice, Tanchum," Touba explained, "but that doesn't mean we lower ourselves to their level to get back at them."

Of course, she was right. Teddy knew it.

"Come with me, we're fixing this," said Simcha.

He took Teddy's hand and led him to the ice cream shop. Teddy heard giggling behind him. His sisters were following. Simcha and Teddy walked to the counter. The old man put his newspaper down. His face showed that he was not surprised to see Teddy again.

Simcha announced, "My son has something to say."

The owner's eyes pierced Teddy. Teddy stood tall, and, in a soft remorseful voice, apologized. Simcha pulled out a few *zloty* from his pocket and placed them on the counter. The sound of coins landing on glass brought finality to the situation.

"Everything has its price," said Simcha, walking out of the shop.

Simcha was a proud father. He was short in stature at five seven with thick, straight black hair. He went out of his way to make sure his children knew right from wrong. Simcha was a dedicated worker who knew and respected the value of hard work. He owned his own business, painting signs for stores around Lodz. On occasion, he brought Teddy along when school was not in session. Teddy was interested in his father's work and meeting the people utilizing his business.

During colder months, Simcha painted home interiors and signs not needed until spring. In warmer months, customers called him the *Kuncenmaller of Lodz*, a specialty painter, as he painted murals for upper-class families. He also prepared stained glass windows for synagogues around town. His work decorated the Stara Shul where his father-in-law had been a former Cantor.

Simcha tried hard to find the right balance between work and family. He would often bring work home, staying up through the night to finish projects. Teddy stayed up too, putting paints on trays for him until his mother told him to go to bed.

Touba was tall for a woman. She was an inch taller than Simcha, and commanded a room's attention. She was a beautiful woman with soft features. Her strawberry blonde hair and blue grey eyes set her apart. Touba was a selfless, nurturing person, always putting her children before herself. She liked cooking but loved to bake. She spent countless hours inventing recipes for meals and cakes using her family as guinea pigs. Most recipes were appetizing, but some would have the kids dropping to the floor, pretending they were poisoned.

On Thursdays, she prepared meals in the local synagogues for the less fortunate. Every Friday, she brought someone new into the home to share in Shabbat.

Back in the apartment after returning from the ice cream parlor, Touba told the children to wash up. Aunt Rose, whom they called Chuh Chuh Rose, and their cousin Cila were coming for dinner. The kids ran to the bathroom and washed their hands and faces. Pola glanced at Teddy making sobbing sounds, rubbing her eyes.

"I'm sorry, I'm sorry, I won't do it again," she teased.

Teddy looked at her, at first irritated, but then he smiled and said, "At least the ice cream was delicious!" He leaned in towards Pola, staring at her. "Wow, that's a bad bruise on your cheek."

"What! There's no bruise," frowned Pola, peering in to the mirror.

Teddy laughed. Realizing he was joking, Pola turned around and gave him a playful shove.

Chuh Chuh Rose was married to Touba's brother and had built a close relationship with Touba over the years. They got together daily and volunteered to help the less fortunate. She was shorter in stature at five three, thin framed and always beautifully dressed. Touba and Rose viewed raising children and the importance of family similarly. They spent days and nights talking about where they saw their children in the future, envisioning doctors, lawyers and a continuation of the family business.

Cila was four years old and a spitting image of her mother. Being the same age as Esther, the cousins were close. They played hide and seek, blocks, and mimicked Pola by trying on her clothes, and using her brushes and makeup. Sometimes Teddy played hide and seek with them. As he was able to get into small hiding places, the girls could spend up to twenty minutes trying to find him.

One day, late in September, Pola and Teddy needed to stop at a specialty paint store for Simcha. He needed powdered colored glass for a porcelain enamel sign. The store was located outside the Jewish Quarter, twenty minutes from their apartment.

Remembering their mother's warning about leaving the Jewish section, Pola and Teddy heightened their senses. Teddy had been to the store before, but this time something felt different. People stared, keeping their distance. Pola noticed a family crossing the street to avoid them. When they arrived, Teddy walked up and said hello to the owner, as he did every time, but the owner ignored him. He continued reading his newspaper and pointed in the direction of Teddy's paint.

Teddy headed to the back. Pola stood, staring in amazement. Their father purchased paints from this man every week. She could not understand why he treated returning customers so rudely.

The store, situated next to a bakery, created a unique aroma of fresh bread, lead-based paint and pastels. The overwhelming scent made Teddy feel dizzy as he approached the cash register to pay. Placing five *zloty* on the counter, Teddy said goodbye and walked outside. The fresh air and pastries next door created a wave of relaxation that traveled from Teddy's head to his toes. He shut his eyes, inhaling deeply, allowing the smell to overtake him.

Pola shoved Teddy, disrupting his brief visit to nirvana. He opened his eyes, and saw what warranted the push. Across the street hung a sign reading, 'Jews are not welcome'. Teddy jumped to a conclusion. He turned to look at the owner of the shop they'd just left. The same sign hung above his front door. He turned to Pola, but before he could speak, she said, "Let's go home."

Pola and Teddy picked up the pace on their walk back. Ten minutes into it, three *goyim* stepped out of an alley to their left. The eldest, fourteen years old and the ringleader, shouted, "What are you doing here, Jews?"

Teddy looked at the teenager, confused.

"I know you're a Jew," he pressed. "I smell you."

The two others approached Pola. The youngest one, around eleven or so, reached up for her head. Pola stepped back but was not fast enough. The boy tugged her wavy black hair violently, dropping her down to one knee. She shrieked, "Let go of me!" but he did not listen. The other boy threw a quarter-sized stone, just missing her left shoulder.

Without hesitating, Teddy reached into his pocket and pulled out the aluminum tube he used to roll his bicycle tire. He forcefully jammed it into the youngest boy's stomach. The boy yelped as he let go of Pola's hair. Teddy reached back and swung a second time, hitting the boy's head. This blow knocked him down to the ground.

Teddy spun around to face the other misfits. He held the aluminum tube in front of him, hovering over Pola, protecting her. The *goyim*, wanting nothing to do with the Jew, ran to their downed friend. Together they lifted him up and headed down the street.

Teddy extended his arm to Pola and helped her up.

"Are you ok?" he asked.

"I'm fine, a little shaken," Pola answered.

She wiped the dirt off her dress and looked at Teddy who peered down the alley, seeing if anyone else approached. Nobody did. Pola tapped Teddy on the shoulder saying, "Tanchum, my hero," her sense of humor returning.

Teddy smiled, half to comfort Pola, half to calm himself. They hugged quickly and hurried home, not stopping for anything.

Back at the apartment, the sight and smell of *golabki* was the best welcome-home gift they could imagine. Sautéed onions and barley mixed with seasoned beef, wrapped in lightly boiled cabbage leaves, made them forget the day's event.

In the kitchen, Chuh Chuh Rose helped Touba cook while Simcha hung his black trench coat up. Cila and Esther played on the kitchen floor with Anka propped up on a cabinet.

"Tanchum!" smiled Cila as he walked through the door. She jumped to her feet and gave him a hug.

"Go wash up," said Chuh Chuh Rose. "Supper is almost ready."

Touba, seeing dirt on Pola's dress and concerned looks on her children's faces, asked what happened.

"We ran into trouble on the way home," said Teddy.

"What kind of trouble?" Simcha chimed in.

"A few boys called us Jews and started a fight," said Pola. "Tanchum scared them away."

"Did they hurt you?" Touba asked, her expression one of horror.

"One pulled my hair," said Pola. "Tanchum got him good and they ran off."

Teddy explained how everything had seemed different. He told his parent how people had avoided them as they headed to the shop, about the many signs hanging in store windows stating that Jews were not welcome, and how the storeowner did not acknowledge them.

"I'll never do business with that man again," vowed Simcha, his voice elevated.

"Who will you get that paint from?" Touba asked.

"I'll find someone else," answered Simcha. He walked up to Pola and Teddy, placing his arms around them. "I'm glad you're both ok."

After supper, the adults sat around the table discussing anti-Semitic occurrences and the harsh changes in politics around Lodz. The children played on the living room floor. Esther held Anka closely. Simcha, looking at Teddy in the living room, spoke to Touba and Rose.

"Can you believe what happened?"

"What is going on in this country?" asked Touba.

"I don't know. I cannot imagine what would have happened to Pola if Tanchum hadn't been there," said Rose.

"I don't want to think about it," answered Touba

"Things can't get any worse," responded Simcha. "They can't."

#

3: Life's Simplicity

Jewish families were accustomed to anti-Semitism in Lodz and had l
many years. They numbered 233,000, roughly a third of the city's po\
and felt safe in large numbers.

Teddy and Pola had now finished school for the year. Esther was also happy it
was the holidays as she would be going to school with her older siblings in the
fall. Of course, Anka was going to attend with her.

In 1939, Simcha's business was at its most prosperous to date. He'd landed a job
refurbishing the stained glass windows in the Stara synagogue. It was going to
take him a year to complete and he relaxed knowing he had definite work
scheduled.

Touba created masterpieces in the kitchen. The smells called out to everyone in
the apartment complex. Her cooking had piqued Pola's interest and she
suddenly started asking questions and wanted to learn the craft.

Esther, now five, decided she'd learned enough about beauty from Pola and
demanded to choose her own clothes and makeup. She pranced around her
bedroom looking more like a clown than a beautiful girl, ignoring her family's
laughs.

It was a good summer for Teddy, who managed to keep out of trouble.
Occasionally, he went into the ice cream shop and bought a cup of vanilla ice
cream. The grumpy storeowner would joke, "I put pieces of mouse *drek* in there
for you."

"Delicious!" was Teddy's usual response, before saying thank you and leaving.

The field across the street was busy from sunrise to sunset, playing host to the
children's imaginations. Some kids played tag. Other children jumped rope or
played soccer. Teddy shouted his Tarzan cry, maneuvering around the field with
fancy footwork, while Chaim and other friends struggled behind him, out of
breath.

The weather was gorgeous. Occasional summer rain passed through, followed
by days of cloudless skies and high temperatures.

...ay, Pola, Chaim and another friend, Avram, walked around Lodz. Piotrkowska Street, the main artery of the city, was only a few blocks away from their apartment. Shops lined the busy road and above them towered the Grand Hotel. Appropriately named, the hotel was the nicest and oldest in Lodz. A person felt luxurious when walking by it. Never able to go inside, the kids stared into the large windows, trying to get a glimpse of the glamour that lay within. Seeing strangers in fancy attire and jewelry threw the children into long episodes of imagining one day being in there with them.

Friday, September 1st was the first day of school. Teddy and Pola complained the entire morning.

"Why do we have to start school on a Friday?" asked Pola.

"Can't we just start on Monday?" Teddy whined.

Esther kept quiet. She was excited to go to school. It was her first day and she'd been waiting impatiently to go for over a year. She contained her excitement, calmly put on her red dress, and made sure Anka was ready to go too.

Touba exclaimed, *"Aylenish mine kinder, youre geyn keyn zayn shpet!"* She was telling the children to hurry up or they'd be late.

"Ema, we're hurrying!" grumbled Pola.

"I'm ready, Ema," said Esther, her voice excited.

Pola felt something wrong in the air on the two-block walk to school.

"Something doesn't feel right," she said.

"What do you mean?" asked Teddy.

He looked around, only seeing children walking.

"I don't know," answered Pola. "Something feels different."

It was common for Pola to have premonitions. She always had a feeling if Teddy hid behind a door waiting to scare her, or if a surprise was in store. One day, Pola had walked by a dress shop with friends and seen a beautiful blue dress with delicate beaded patterns. She fell in love with it and knew it was hers. When she got home later that day, the dress was on her bed. Touba had picked it up as a surprise for her birthday.

Esther was abnormally quiet; her nerves finally got to her. Her grip on Anka tightened as the school came into view. Older children stood outside the front door talking about their summer experiences, while younger children apprehensively kept their heads down and walked inside. Teddy saw some friends and decided to stay with them until school started. Pola walked Esther inside, making sure she found her classroom before heading towards her own.

The first day of school was uneventful. It was a lot of catching up with old friends or meeting people new to the area. Teachers did not hand out schoolwork under the same pretext Pola and Teddy had whined about earlier: school should not have started on Friday.

At the end of the day, Teddy, Pola and Esther met up by the main entrance to walk home.

Pola turned to Esther. "How was it?"

"Good," Esther replied. She liked her teacher and knew a few children in her class, which had made her day more comfortable.

Something still did not feel right to Pola. The two-block walk home did not have the same hustle and bustle. It felt empty. A few stores usually open until late had closed early. The trolleys appeared to have stopped for the day.

What is going on? she thought to herself.

They turned on Mielczarskiego Street and noticed the ice cream shop was closed. The front door to their apartment was open, wedged by a rock that must have taken two people to move it. The children climbed the stairwell, only making it to the second floor before the sweet smell of *kugel* slapped Teddy's nostrils. The egg noodle casserole made with farmer's cheese, eggs, cinnamon, raisons, sour cream, butter and sugar had always been a favorite of his. His newfound energy helped him climb the stairs two at a time and race through the front door of his apartment.

Pola and Esther arrived shortly after. The scene they expected was not the one they saw. Simcha must have closed shop early too because he was home. His paints and a few pieces of wood were lying on the living room floor, signifying he had been there for some time. Chuh Chuh Rose sat at the dining room table, one hand on her lap, the other supporting her head as she leaned on it with a distressed look.

Touba moved frantically around the kitchen trying to cook dinner. Her hands shook violently as she tried to control the pan, paying no attention to the food falling on the floor. The radio in the living room played loudly and the children heard the message their family had been hearing.

"We have an important announcement to make. At 4:45 this morning, September 1st 1939, the Germans crossed into our territory. The German Air Force has attacked our army and invaded Polish territory. The German Air Force has attacked many towns within Poland…"

"Go wash up for supper," Simcha interrupted, trying to act normal.

"Yes, Abba," Pola responded, pushing Teddy and Esther towards the bathroom.

As the children washed up, Pola looked over at Teddy.

"Did you hear that?" she asked.

"Yes," Teddy responded, wrapping his head around what he had just heard.

"Hear what?" asked Esther.

"Nothing, Esther, let's go and eat," smiled Pola, leading her to the dining room.

The smell of freshly-baked *kugel* made Teddy forget about the broadcast for a second, but he soon remembered as the radio continued to run messages from emergency channels.

Voices emanating from the radio overpowered the familiar clings and clangs of silverware on porcelain plates. A recorded message played repeatedly, only changing for brief updates that never seemed positive for Poland. Nobody said a word but everyone thought the same thing. What is happening?

After dinner, the family prepared for Shabbat. Esther brought out candles: the customary two representing the two commandments – Zachor, to remember, and Shamor, to observe – and three additional candles which Touba lit for her three children.

Simcha turned off the lights twenty minutes before sundown and, lastly, the radio. The room fell eerily silent. Everyone felt a sudden disconnect from the world and the events happening. It appeared everyone in the community felt the same. The only sound they could hear was the gently blowing wind outside the living room window, gracefully passing by, like the angel of death.

With eighteen minutes to go until sunset, Touba began. She lit the candles and said a prayer that they'd all heard hundreds of times.

"Barukh atah Adonai Eloheinu, melekh ha'olam, asher kid'shanu b'mitzvotav v'tzivanu l'hadlik ner shel Sha-bos ko-desh." Blessed are You, Lord our God, King of the Universe, who has sanctified us with His commandments, and commanded us to kindle the light of the holy Shabbat.

After acknowledging the Sabbath, the children played in the living room. Teddy was catching up on his newest Tarzan adventure and letting his imagination take him swinging on the vines in a far-off jungle. Esther combed Anka's hair while Pola sat on the couch staring out the living room window.

I knew something was going to happen, she thought, sighing as she wondered about their unknown future.

The adults at the table shared her feelings.

"What are we to do?" asked Touba.

"Too early to decide," answered Simcha.

"This may be the end of life as we know it," said Rose.

"Why would you say that?" responded Simcha.

"You've heard the laws against Jews in Germany," said Rose, the fear coming through her voice.

"I have faith in our army," said Simcha as the candlelight cast a looming shadow on the wall behind him. "We'll be ok," he continued, trying to provide reassurance.

He looked over at his children playing in the living room.

I hope we will be, he thought.

#

4: September March On Lodz

"Are they going to be ok?" asked Hayden.

"What, honey?" I responded, thrown off by her question.

"They're going to be ok, right?" she asked again.

"I can't tell you now, it'll ruin the story," I replied.

"I just want them all to be ok," Hayden continued.

"You'll find out soon enough," I explained, "but I can tell you now, if you really want."

"No, it's ok," said Hayden. "I guess I'll wait."

Traffic was at a standstill with no sign of movement. Rain continued to come down in sheets, dropping visibility to almost zero.

Shannon reached out and grabbed my right hand which was resting on the center console. I looked over and saw her smiling back – a silent assent to my narrative. It was her way of confirming I was doing fine. She had not heard the story either.

#

Fear engulfed Lodz. In an effort to maintain some sense of normalcy, the Znamirowskis continued to go to school. Each day, fewer children attended class. Frequent reports of approaching German troops packed the radio waves. Shops and factories remained open but workers raced home to be with their families. They huddled around radios, praying for good news but only hearing the worst.

Simcha, Touba, Rose and other adults in the apartment building discussed their options daily. Should they stay in Lodz and risk occupation under strict, hateful anti-Semitic laws? Should they leave? Where would they go? How would they survive on their own when nobody offered help?

Radio reports made it sound as though Germans troops were everywhere, describing them as an invincible and unstoppable force. Teddy was terrified at the thought of running into a German soldier.

The Znamirowskis decided to stay as the risk of venturing into the unknown was too dangerous, even compared to occupation. With extensive rumors of labor camps, leaving Lodz appeared to come with an immediate consequence.

A handful of families in the apartment complex fled. They were willing to take their chances out in the world rather than wait and see what the Germans had planned for them. They collected their valuables, and packed their suitcases with as much as they could carry. Some families had relatives upon whom they could rely, though many in their desperation thought that being anywhere else was a better bet than Lodz. Emotional goodbyes gave way to fates unknown. Nobody heard from them again.

In a matter of days, residents heard cannon fire from south of the city, bringing a sense of reality to their situation. While radio reports were one thing, feeling thunderous booms from weapons created to kill was quite another. As each minute passed, the concussive sounds of cannons grew louder, creating a crescendo of fear within the citizens of Lodz.

The Znamirowski family crowded together, kneeling on the wooden floor in their parents' bedroom. It was the furthest room from the horrifying sounds outside.

"Don't worry, Anka, we'll be ok," said Esther, trying more to convince herself than the doll.

Touba wrapped her arms around the children, holding them tightly, while Simcha's arms held her. Though the bombardment never came close, the horrific sound made it seem as though the shells were landing next door. The concussions tapered off and eventually ceased.

"What's happening?" asked Pola.

"I don't know, *mine sheyn ponem*," said Simcha.

"I hope we won," said Teddy, standing up and acting brave.

He ran to the window hoping to see the aftermath. He could not. Whatever happened was far from their fourth-floor apartment.

Touba yelled at him to get back, fearful something else would happen.

"Sorry, Ema" Teddy answered, running back towards the room's center. Simcha lightly smacked the back of Teddy's head when he got within reach. A look that said "What were you thinking?" clouded Simcha's face.

The children stayed in their parents' bedroom that night, afraid the next attack would happen within the walls of Lodz. Touba woke up throughout the night to check on her family, to make sure they were safe, and they were – for now. There were no signs of imminent danger.

The morning of September 8th brought strange sounds to the streets of Lodz. Teddy turned to see Touba, Pola and Esther still sleeping, no doubt exhausted from the restless night. He tiptoed to his room, threw on brown trousers with a white button-down shirt and headed for the front door.

Simcha's voice stopped him in his tracks.

"Where do you think you're going?" he said, sipping a fresh cup of coffee in the dining room.

"I want to see what's going on," Teddy replied, startled.

"Come, we'll go together," said Simcha, interested himself.

They ran down the stairs and headed outside. Mielczarskiego Street was empty but it sounded like everyone was over towards Piotrkowska. They turned right onto Gdanska and then left onto Legionow. With every step, the noise of the crowd grew louder. They crossed over Zachodnia. People gathered in the streets to observe the commotion.

"What's going on, Abba?" Teddy asked.

"I don't know, Tanchum," Simcha answered, looking ahead.

The crowd in front of them was thick and made seeing the street impossible. They approached Liberty Square, where Piotrkowska and Legionow intersected. Simcha lifted Teddy onto his shoulders to get a better view.

"What do you see, Tanchum?" Simcha asked.

As Teddy looked over the mob, he saw his answer. It was not good.

The unfamiliar sound was black leather, front-laced German army boots hitting pavement as they marched on Lodz. Soldiers lined up as far as Teddy's eyes could see. They walked tall, kicking their feet out in front of them, each step in complete unison. They appeared superhuman. Who were these men, these conquerors of Lodz? More importantly, what did they want? What did they intend to do?

The soldiers held an array of weapons. Rifles looked like extended venomous snakes reaching for their prey. Germans who grasped machine-guns scared Teddy the most. They wore belts of ammunition around their necks like prized teeth of those they killed.

Tanks passed by, bearing the iron cross on their sides. Engines roared like evil dragons as thick black smoke billowed from them. Caravans of trucks carrying endless loads of superhuman soldiers continued driving by. The smell of diesel was overwhelming and made Teddy nauseous.

Teddy had never seen anything like the spectacle before him and he was terrified. He had heard his parents and neighbors speak about the evil Germans and their unacceptable mistreatment of Jews, but he'd assumed it was just rumors. Now the Germans were in Lodz and the mere sight of them sent waves of fear flooding through Teddy, paralyzing him.

Sounds of the crowd grew louder as the citizens of Lodz continued arriving. Endless Germans marched. The sound of mixed conversations from hundreds of people came together into one uniform chant: "*Heil Hitler.*"

Confused by what he heard, Teddy turned to his right. The crowd was not against the Germans, they were cheering them. Teddy witnessed people saluting the marching invaders with outstretched right arms.

Simcha did not have to see what was happening: hearing it was enough. He took Teddy down from his shoulders, grabbed his hand, and walked briskly back to the apartment.

"Abba, what's happening?" Teddy asked.

"Something horrible, Tanchum" said Simcha. "We need to get home."

#

5: Nobody Is Safe

Back at the apartment, the girls were up and dressed. Touba was in the kitchen putting a pot of *chulnt* together for dinner the next night. The front door swung open.

"Come everyone! We need to pack our belongings," said Simcha.

"What's going on?" asked Touba, concerned.

"The Germans have occupied our city and have support from the masses," he answered, sounding angry and apprehensive.

"Where will we go?" asked Touba.

"Nowhere yet," Simcha replied. "First we must wait and see, but we must prepare, just in case."

Lodz's situation declined rapidly over the next few days. The Znamirowskis tried to maintain their routine to keep life as normal as possible. The children went to school despite the sharp decline in attendance. To avoid entangling in any disturbing situations, the children ran to and from school every day.

On one occasion, the children headed to school and witnessed a Hasidic man in his thirties carrying books to work. Two German soldiers appeared and bumped into him, making him drop some of his books. The man bent down to pick them up but the soldier continued to knock the rest of the books out of his hands and laugh. The Hasidic man retrieved his books and tried walking away, only enraging the soldier further. The German began pushing the Jew around when his initial attempts to provoke him did not provide the desired response.

Repeatedly, he rose to his feet, unwilling to let German soldiers defeat him. The other soldier grew tired of the game. The Hasidic man rose to his feet, exhausted, and received a blow to the back of his head from a rifle.

"*Oy Gevalt*," said Pola, gasping at the sight.

The soldier gave a second blow. Blood pooled onto the sidewalk and the Hasidic man did not get back up. The children ran to school without looking back.

"Why would they hit that man?" asked Esther, running through the front door.

"Because they're evil," Pola responded.

The kids separated and went to their sparsely-attended classes, trying to lose themselves in school and wash away the memory of what they had witnessed.

The Jew was not on the sidewalk as the children ran by on their way home from school. In his place, they could see a small pool of dried blood trailing into an alleyway.

When the children got home, they told their parents what they had witnessed. Touba wrapped her arms around them, glad they were safe and whispered, "I love you."

She turned to look at Simcha and asked, "What should we do?"

Simcha shrugged his shoulders, not having an answer for her. He leaned in, putting his hands around his family and told them, "We'll get through this."

A day later was the high holy day of Rosh Hashanah. The holiday symbolized the Jewish New Year and was the first of the high holy days in Judaism. It represented the day God created Adam and Eve and their understanding of humankind's role under God. It was a day of self-reflection and prayer.

The Znamirowskis enjoyed Rosh Hashanah. It was a day the family got together and welcomed the New Year. They had relatives over for dinner. They began with prayer, and then ate apples dipped in honey, symbolizing the beginning of a sweet, happy year.

After dinner, the family headed to the Stara Shul to attend prayer. Teddy's favorite part was the blowing of the Shofar. The traditional ram's horn sounded like a trumpet and blew at different intervals denoting the arrival of a new year.

This year, however, there would be no Rosh Hashanah. In 1939, the Nazis made it mandatory for all synagogues to close for the high holy holiday and made Jewish businesses and schools remain open.

Hearing the news, Simcha was furious.

"How can they go against God's will!" he yelled. "They will be punished for this!"

Touba tried to console him, telling him everything would be all right and back to normal soon.

"You mean we're not going to hear the Shofar?" asked Teddy.

"No," Simcha went on, "because of those shmucks outside. They can *kush mine tuches*." They could kiss his ass indeed.

"*Shah* Simcha, they may hear you," whispered Touba.

That evening the Znamirowskis made their own Rosh Hashanah service in their apartment. They spoke softly so soldiers passing by would not hear anything. They ate sweet foods and dipped their apples, hoping for better times and a Rosh Hashanah the following year.

Simcha made a fist with his hand and blew through it, giving his best attempt at a Shofar. Teddy laughed, appreciating the effort. Touba sat back and watched her family. *As long as we are together*, she thought.

The children ran to school the next day. A German soldier was standing at the front door, which took them by surprise. He was there ensuring the school remained open and students attended. It was the first time since the invasion that the classrooms were full.

Esther, young and naïve, held Anka close to her chest. She inhaled deeply and walked up to the soldier.

"*Shanah Tovah*." She wished the imposing individual holding a semi-automatic machine gun a Happy New Year.

"Piss off," replied the soldier.

Esther lowered her head and rushed into the school.

"Don't speak to them," Pola reminded Esther. "You don't want them to notice you."

Life was spiraling out of control in Lodz. Rules and regulations instituted by the Nazis grew more strict and cruel every day. Simcha was hardest hit out of the Znamirowski family. Jews could no longer use public transportation so Simcha made the 2.5-kilometer return trip to his business each day on foot. If he ran late, he took Teddy's bicycle to help him get there faster.

During his commute, Simcha continually saw Nazis demoralizing people on the streets. Germans lined up Jews on sidewalks and made them dance or act like monkeys while they harassed them, shooting bullets at their feet.

Beatings by the side of the road were common, as were soldiers cutting off a man's *payos*, shaving off his beard or peeing on his *yarmulke* or *shtreimels*. Occasionally, people were hanged from trees. Their lifeless bodies blew effortlessly with the wind. Their hands down by their sides, heads tilted in inhuman positions. Simcha crossed to the opposite side of the street to keep his distance from the evil happening, and tried not to draw attention to himself.

Like all Jewish business owners in Lodz, Simcha had to place a sign in front of his shop declaring that a Jew owned it. Simcha was a sign maker and, in his own little way of standing up to the Germans, he painted a beautiful sign and hung it for everyone to see. When asked why he put so much effort into a sign that put him down, he replied, "I'm a sign maker; this is a perfect way to advertise." Trying, as always, to make the best of any situation.

Over the next weeks, the German presence increased. Soldiers stood guard by Jewish businesses making sure non-Jews did not conduct business with Jews. A few business owners refused to obey the law and received quick judgment with a single gunshot.

One day, Simcha walked to work and noticed a small crowd had formed outside his building. As he approached, he realized that German soldiers had vandalized his shop. The windows were all broken and the door had been kicked in. They had destroyed most of the supplies. Paint was everywhere. The most damage was to canvas, wood, tin and other materials Simcha used to make his signs.

Jews in the crowd shook their heads in disgust at the sight of another robbed business. Most of them had black eyes and bruises from dealing with the vandalism of their own shops. Poles and Germans in the crowd pointed and laughed at the demise of another Jewish business. Some of them pushed Jews out of the way to get an unobstructed view of the destruction.

Simcha entered his shop and stood in the doorway for a few seconds, trying to piece together what he saw in front of him. *Why would they do this?* he wondered. A tear formed in his eye when he thought about the hard work and sacrifice that had gone into creating the shop.

The business had started in their apartment before Teddy and Esther were born. What eventually became Teddy's bedroom was originally Simcha's workshop. People in town knew his artistic talent, and, wanting to help a friend, came to him to have their signs redone. As more people saw his work, the business grew quickly. Orders became back orders, and Simcha needed to expand. He chose the location of his shop strategically and planned on growing his name and reaching out to a bigger community. On opening day, fifteen new orders had come in and it was clear that Simcha had picked his location correctly. From that point on, business flourished. It was the family's livelihood.

He stepped further into the store. Sounds of broken glass under his shoes pained him. Smells of fresh paint and supplies that had, up until that moment, brought him joy and happiness, now brought him despair. He bent down and started to pick up any materials he thought might be salvageable.

What am I going to do? How am I going to provide for my family? These were just a few of the thoughts running through Simcha's mind. Even in the face of despair, he was creative and a survivor, like all Znamirowskis. He knew he would find a way.

The soldiers who'd destroyed his shop had not managed to take any of the profits. Every day as Simcha closed his shop, he stuffed money into his socks and shoes, always leaving his pockets empty in case somebody wanted to rob him. He took the cash home where he hid it under a loose floorboard in his bedroom, preferring to manage the money himself rather than depositing it into a bank he did not trust.

Simcha spent the rest of the day making trips between the apartment and his shop, transferring usable supplies and enduring constant heckling from non-Jews. On his last trip, he looked to the left of the entryway and saw something he had walked past all day and never noticed. The beautiful sign he painted indicating a Jew owned the business now bore a swastika with '*Judenfrei*' – free of Jews – written underneath it.

Back at the apartment, Simcha set up his sign shop in the living room. Luckily, he still had most of the supplies needed to continue his job for the Stara Synagogue stained glass windows. However, the terrorizing of Jewish businesses did not leave too many owners looking to refurbish their signs and, as a result, Simcha's work ground to a halt.

As the children hurried home from school each day, the Lodz they knew was now unrecognizable. Jews were frequently terrorized in the streets. Many Jewish businesses tried staying open but the extreme laws against them made it nearly impossible. Hatred was palpable and filled the air around them.

Pola, Teddy, Esther, Cila and Chaim were walking a block away from the Znamirowski apartment. As they walked shoulder to shoulder, making sure to avoid eye contact with everyone, they caught the attention of a German soldier standing nearby.

The familiar sound of black leather boots on cobblestone made Teddy's heart jump. The soldier lengthened his stride until he was right on top of them.

"Kommen heir." The soldier shouted at them to come here. The children, hoping he was speaking to someone else, quickened their pace.

"Kommen jetzt heir!" He yelled again, his voice right on top of them.

At once, all five children stopped and, trembling, they turned around. The German stood tall. He looked the children up and down, inspecting them. He paced back and forth, each step filling them with fear. He stopped in front of Chaim, leaning in close to his face.

"Wie viele kekse hast du heute essen?" The soldier asked him how many cookies he'd eaten today. Seeing the confused look on Chaim's face made it clear to the soldier that the boy did not understand his superior language. He stepped back, looking around to see if he had any spectators, and fixed his uniform. The soldier screamed, *"Dummer Jude,"* stupid Jew, and lodged his boot into Chaim's stomach. Chaim fell immediately to his knees, gasping for air. Slowly, he leaned over and lay on the street curled up in the fetal position, groaning.

The soldier began pacing in front of the children again, finally stopping in front of Esther who clutched onto Anka in absolute panic. He crouched in front of her and stared. When their eyes met, the soldier whispered, "This is the real reason I stopped you." He reached over and removed Anka from her arms. "My daughter will love this back in Germany."

Tears welled up in Esther's eyes as she realized Anka's fate. The German casually stood up, oblivious to the emotional distress he was causing the five-year-old girl. He turned to walk away, but as he stepped, a voice stopped him.

"Give it back," Teddy said, in perfect German.

The soldier turned to face Teddy, who clenched his fists tightly. As the German approached, Teddy silently prayed he'd made the right choice in speaking up.

"So you speak German, do you?" said the soldier.

"Yes, sir, it's a great language. I had to learn it," answered Teddy, hoping that sucking up to him would ease the situation.

"It's the only language," the German answered. "You're lucky you speak it so well."

Teddy never saw the rifle butt coming. The blow to his head knocked him flat on his back. As he lay there staring at the open sky, everything suddenly went dark.

#

6: Lodz No Longer

"Saba doesn't die, you know," I said, looking in the rearview mirror.

"Huh? Oh, I know!" Hayden answered.

"Well, I'm just telling you because you look concerned," I continued.

"I'm not concerned, but I don't like mean people," responded Hayden.

"It was a different time, sweetheart," I explained, "Germany suffered after World War I and needed something to bring them out of their depression. Unfortunately, the wrong man stepped up for the job, and instead of giving the people of Germany something to believe in, he gave them something to blame their problems on."

"You mean Hitler blaming the Jews?" Hayden asked.

"Exactly," I answered.

Hayden took a deep breath, letting out a casual sigh. She leaned back in her seat and looked out her window. As I continued the story, Hayden listened intently, allowing her imagination to take over.

#

"Tanchum, Tanchum wake up," a muffled voice said. "Please Tanchum, wake up," he heard again.

Teddy slowly opened his eyes to a blurry world. He looked around the room, squinting to see clearly. His head throbbed with each attempt to move his eyes. When his sight returned, he was no longer looking up at the sky but at a ceiling in an unfamiliar room.

The soldier had knocked Teddy unconscious. Pola, Chaim, Esther and Cila had struggled to pull him to the apartment. When they got there, Cila, already out of breath from dragging him, ran upstairs to tell Simcha what happened. Simcha and Touba had barreled out of the apartment to find Teddy on the ground, out cold.

With ease, Simcha lifted Teddy's light, lifeless body onto his shoulder and carried him to a family friend, Dr. Daniel, a general practitioner a few blocks away. Dr. Daniel laid Teddy down on his bed, listened to his heart and lungs and applied cold meat to the welt forming on his head. He explained to them that Teddy would be fine but would have a terrible headache when he awoke.

Teddy's vision eventually cleared. He peered around and saw his family surrounding him, looking concerned. Teddy smiled and shrugged his shoulders as if to say, "It's me, what do you expect?" He turned his head, trying to cope with the terrible throbbing, and saw Esther. For a split second, his headache disappeared when he saw Anka in her arms. His gamble had paid off. He straightened his head, shut his eyes, and drifted off to sleep.

A few hours later, Teddy awoke. Once he was finally able to sit upright, the throbbing became unbearable. He crouched forward, placing his hands over his head, and sat there until the pounding subsided.

He heard the worried muffled voices of his family and Dr. Daniel through the bedroom door.

"Why would he do that?"

"It's just a doll."

"How could he do that to a child?"

"How much longer will this last?"

Teddy stood up and cautiously walked towards the door. Reaching it, he rested a hand on it to brace himself and inhaled deeply. He opened the door and walked into the living room.

Everyone sat on couches waiting for him. Pola and Esther kneeled on the floor by the fireplace. Esther held up Anka, showing Teddy she was grateful. Chaim was hunched over in a wooden table chair with compressed, iced meat over his dark, bruised stomach. The imprint of the soldier's boot was emblazoned into his soft belly. He self-medicated with freshly fried *khruchikis*. The airy cookie crunched with each bite and left a trail of crumbs and powdered sugar on his sweater.

Simcha and Touba sat on a couch facing the fireplace, and turned when they heard the door creak. Both were relieved to see Teddy up and moving again.

Touba asked, "Tanchum, are you ok?"

Nodding yes, Teddy came over to the couch and sat next to them.

"How long have I been sleeping?" Teddy questioned.

"About four hours now," Dr. Daniel answered.

"What time is it?" Teddy asked.

"Quarter after eight," responded Simcha.

Curfew set by the Nazis did not allow Jews to be out of their homes between 8pm and 6am. As such, the Znamirowskis and Chaim would have to spend the night at Dr. Daniel's.

Dr. Daniel's wife, Miriam, cooked dinner in the kitchen. Touba offered to help but was immediately hushed.

"Yes, you can help by sitting and making yourself comfortable," answered Miriam.

Smells emanating from the kitchen wafted into the living room, making everyone's stomachs grumble in anticipation. When the announcement came that dinner was ready, they all got up and moved quickly into the dining room.

To their amazement, a huge meal waited for them.

"I'm glad I didn't fill up on cookies!" Chaim exclaimed, gazing at the feast in front of him.

Miriam's dinner began with a bowl of *grochowka*, pea soup made extra thick the way Teddy liked it. Dinner moved on to *golabki* and ended with more *khruchikis* fresh off the pan.

Miriam apologized throughout the meal for not having enough food, explaining that she'd had to cook it on short notice.

"You're crazy," Touba laughed, "There's more than enough food for everyone and it's all delicious, thank you."

The family remained around the dinner table after supper, the adults drinking tea and discussing recent events while the children continued eating cookies.

"Did you hear about the great synagogue?" asked Dr. Daniel.

"Such a shame," Touba responded, shaking her head in disgust. "What's this world coming to?"

"I don't know, but I fear it is far from over," Simcha added.

Teddy, suddenly not feeling well, left the table and lay on the couch. He stared at the fireplace for a few minutes. The flames covering the burning wood mesmerized him, each one dancing a hypnotic rhythm that drew him into a deep sleep. Vivid nightmares, appearing as a mixture of recent experiences and things that had not yet happened, plagued Teddy's sleep.

Teddy ran down a hallway of his school. Hearing something behind him, he turned around. A boy was chasing him. On second glance, Teddy saw he was the boy who had pulled Pola's hair a few weeks earlier. Teddy continued to run, never reaching the end of the hallway, which was lengthening in front of his eyes. Every time he neared the exit, the corridor extended.

Finally, reaching the exit door, he pushed hard but it would not budge. He thrust his body frantically into it but to no avail. Looking over his shoulder, Teddy expected the boy to be right on top of him, but he was gone.

He turned to give the door another push but it had vanished. Teddy was no longer in the school but at the park across from his house. Children played soccer and tag all around him. In the distance, a mass formed down Mielczarskiego Street. The mass grew larger, moving closer. A familiar noise accompanied it.

Teddy trembled on hearing the boots of one thousands marching soldiers. *Why are they marching on my street*? Children playing soccer stopped to stare. One by one, they dropped to the ground, lifeless.

The grumpy man from the ice cream shop ran outside, yelling at the soldiers to leave. Teddy saw his ice cream-filled beard partially cut off and accented by two black eyes. Teddy felt a tug at his pant leg. He looked down and saw a mouse staring back up.

He could not understand what he was witnessing. Teddy bent over to pick up the mouse. Standing back up, he was no longer in the field, but an area of Lodz he did not visit frequently. The area looked different. It seemed desolate. Everything, covered in a shade of gray, appeared filthy. People wandered with no purpose to their life. Beggars littered the streets. People walked past them, ignoring their presence.

German soldiers were everywhere. Teddy snuck around but as he crept into an alleyway, one spotted him. The soldier called out to Teddy. He turned around, and, as they made eye contact, took off running.

The soldier chased Teddy down the alleyway but he was too fast. He took a sharp left and sprinted down another passage leading to an open area, overcrowded with Jews. Teddy disappeared into the crowd. Looking back, the soldier was nowhere in sight.

Teddy navigated his way through the crowd and saw Touba and Esther in the distance. They waited in a line to board a truck. People everywhere were crying. Touba held on to Esther, who in turn clung to Anka. Seeing the German driver and the swastika on the side of the truck, Teddy screamed at them to get out of the line but his words were mere whispers. No matter how hard he yelled, he could not produce an audible sound. Teddy ran to the truck but arrived too late. They had boarded and were en route.

German soldiers turned to the crowd with angry faces and eyes wide with hate. Simultaneously, they aimed their weapons at innocent people and opened fire. Screams of fear and pain arose from the crowd as it dispersed. Complete chaos overwhelmed the area.

Teddy found he could not move. His legs felt as heavy as lead and it was impossible to take a step. He lost his breath, straining to get away. Then the firing stopped. The silence was terrifying. Everyone was gone except for Teddy and the soldiers staring at him with menacing looks.

Behind the soldiers, Teddy saw a fire consuming a few buildings. Curious to see what he was looking at, the soldiers turned around. A flash of light followed by a thunderous boom knocked everyone down to the ground. Before Teddy could stand back up, another bang sent him flying through the air.

#

Teddy woke up from his nightmare covered in sweat and shivering furiously. His clothes were soaked through. He rolled over to see the fire still lit. To his surprise, everyone was awake, despite the clock on the wall reading 1am. They crowded the living room windows and were staring outside.

What's so interesting? Teddy wondered.

He stood up from the couch, still shivering, and wrapped himself in a blanket. He took a moment to warm himself by the fire then headed to the window.

Teddy could not believe his eyes. The sight in front of him was unfathomable. Flames engulfed the Stara Synagogue. The wind picked up in their direction and the heat of the fire burned their faces. All of Lodz heard the crackling of wood and the shattering of glass. The blaze lit up the streets as if it were daytime.

A crowd gathered on the street to watch, most likely Poles or Germans. Jews would not risk being out past curfew or they would meet the same fate as the synagogue. The temple began to crumble due to the extreme temperatures inside. Firefighters showed up for crowd control and to ensure the fire did not spread to surrounding structures.

"First the great synagogue, now the Stara," said Dr. Daniel shaking his head in disbelief.

"They're trying to burn us out," answered Simcha, his voice enraged. "I hope no one was inside."

"What are you going to do for work, Abba?" asked Pola.

Simcha looked at the synagogue. The fire cracked, smashed and burned every window. Places where windows once existed were now unrecognizable because of the building's collapse.

It had not occurred to Simcha until that moment that he was now officially out of work. All his other avenues of business had dried up with the strict laws applied by the Nazis. The Stara was the one job he'd been counting on for the tough times ahead. The Znamirowskis now relied on what little money they had on hand and on prayer for better things to come.

"We'll find a way," answered Simcha.

People screamed on the street as two Germans forced a line-up. From the apartment, you could see one soldier pacing back and forth, giving a lecture. He started walking away before stopping and abruptly turning back around. A series of gunshots went off and the line of bodies fell unnaturally to the ground. Touba reached down to cover Esther's eyes as she gasped in horror. One by one, the Germans threw the bodies into the burning synagogue and walked away.

"What were they doing out past curfew?" said Simcha, assuming the unlucky people were Jews.

"Who knows," answered Dr. Daniel.

The next day, the smell of the burned synagogue was overwhelming. Smoke cleared from the scene and Jews from around the area climbed through the ruins to see if anything was salvageable. Everything was gone. Fragments of chairs and a stone carving of a Star of David were among the only things that remained. Germans and Poles chuckled under their breath as they walked past the burned Jewish house of God.

Adding insult to injury, Jews were ordered to wear an armband on their right arm indicating they were Jewish. Now impossible to blend in with society, they became easy targets. Any Jew caught not wearing their armband faced dire consequences.

A month later, the armband changed to a yellow Star of David worn on both the front and back of their clothing.

The Znamirowskis coped as best they could over the next few months. The children continued school, still running both ways to avoid confrontation. Touba volunteered within the community and experimented with her cooking. Simcha rarely left the house. Occasionally work came his way but the outside world had become too dangerous for a man his age.

Daily round-ups occurred in Lodz to recruit for forced heavy labor. Jews dug trenches, moved rocks, and shoveled snow – anything the Germans could think up to make them work. More often than not, fewer men returned from the day's work than went out. If they were lucky enough to return at the day's end, bruises covered their bodies from beatings they'd received.

Stories circulated around the Jewish community about what happened to the vanishing men. If someone stopped working to rest, he had two options according to the German who confronted him. The better option, which occurred if the soldier was in a good mood, was a beating, often leaving the person severely injured. The second option, death, only came after a beating.

The Germans had many ways to take a person's life. Often, they found a tree nearby, strung a noose to it and hanged the person while forcing fellow laborers to watch him expire. They left the body there as a reminder of what happened to those who needed a "break".

Other times, Germans forced the worker to dig a shallow hole. The man sobbed with a foreboding sense of what he was doing. The worker would plead with the soldier to allow him to work but the German would not have it. When the hole was complete, the person kneeled in front of it. A bullet to the head sent his lifeless body into the shallow grave. Everyone went back to work except for one or two men who stayed behind to cover the body.

True hate had permeated Lodz. Germans beat Jews and looted their shops daily. Poles took full advantage of the German occupation and used it as an excuse to act on their hatred. Crimes upon Jews went unpunished. Everyone suffered, unable to hide the Star of David on their clothes, and some more than others depending on how 'Jewish' they appeared.

In the beginning of 1940, a message went through Lodz explaining that infectious diseases had contaminated Baluty, the northern quarter of the city, and the people who lived there needed to evacuate.

A few weeks later, another message went out stating that Jews were to relocate into Baluty and had a month to do so. Simcha sat at the kitchen table when he read the notice. Slamming his hand down on the table, he screamed, "How can they do this to us?"

"Do what, Abba?" Pola asked.

"They are kicking us out of our house and making us move to Baluty," Simcha answered.

"But isn't Baluty contaminated?" asked Touba.

"They're trying to kill us all off!" Simcha said, enraged.

"When do we need to leave?" asked Touba.

"We have a month," said Simcha "but we're not going anywhere until they make us. Maybe they won't follow through."

The Germans instructed that the Jews were to bring only what they could carry. In preparation, Simcha and Teddy went out and purchased two sleds to help load and drag their belongings if they were forced to move.

As the days went by, people continued carrying their belongings past the Znamirowski apartment. Horse and mule-drawn carts loaded with people's livelihoods headed north to Baluty. Sleds piled high with food and clothes made slow progress. Children and adults alike struggled to pull them through the cobblestone streets.

Simcha stood next to Teddy at the window and looked out at them on the street below.

"This is how I envision the exodus," said Simcha.

Teddy let out a small chuckle under his breath.

"I was thinking that too," he responded.

"Let's hope this passes and we can remain here in our home," said Simcha.

"I hope so," answered Teddy.

People from all walks of life passed the apartment like a herd of buffalo migrating to greener pasture. Sadly, the pasture was not greener where they were going.

Old men on crutches hobbled next to younger men, who were hunched over from the weight of heavy sacks on their backs. Mentally ill people walked next to their caregivers, some screaming obscenities while others twitched and shook, occasionally hitting themselves.

There were older men next to younger boys and ugly women walking next to beautiful girls. Some couples held hands while others covered their faces, crying. Everyone walked at the same slow pace, prolonging the journey, as if not yet being at their destination made things somehow better.

The beginning of March came quicker than anticipated. Teddy awoke and slowly sat up in bed. Still groggy, he walked over to his window to check the weather. Snow had fallen the night before. A thin layer of pure white covered the streets and rooftops of the surrounding buildings. The field across the street looked like one big puff of cream. Everything seemed peaceful.

How beautiful, Teddy thought.

As he walked to his dresser, he heard screams and a gunshot in the distance. Shaking off the now common sounds, Teddy continued rifling through his dresser.

A few moments later, the screams and gunshots increased.

What's going on? Teddy wondered.

The sounds grew louder as they approached the Znamirowski apartment. A woman ran down the street shouting, "They're coming, run!"

Screaming now came from inside the apartment building. Teddy was heading back to the window when he heard a knock at the front door.

Simcha was sitting at the kitchen table reading the newspaper. He also heard the screams and the knock. Slowly, he folded up the paper and headed for the door. As he reached for the handle, the German on the other side kicked it open.

Stunned from the force of the door, Simcha stood there staring down the barrel of a rifle.

"Fifteen minutes, then get the hell out," the German screamed.

#

7: Eviction

"Touba, we need to go now!" Simcha shouted, running frantically around the apartment and packing their important belongings.

"What's going on?" Touba answered.

"A piece-of-*drek* Nazi kicked our door in and told me to be out of here in fifteen minutes," Simcha responded.

"What if we don't go in fifteen minutes?" asked Touba, herself now packing whatever she could grab.

"We won't be here to find out," Simcha answered quickly.

Luckily, the family had packed their bags a few months earlier when deciding to stay or leave Lodz. Teddy ran downstairs and readied the two sleds to load them up with as many things as they could bear.

Good thing it snowed last night, he thought.

The girls were upstairs throwing whatever they could grab into boxes. Teddy and Simcha made several trips bringing suitcases and boxes, which represented their entire lives, to the sleds.

"Come on! We have five minutes!" Simcha yelled in a panic.

Shots echoed through halls and stairwells of neighboring apartment buildings. People were fleeing their homes – running for their lives. The screams were piercing and seemingly endless.

The family exited the building and stepped into complete chaos. People ran in every direction. Men pulled sleds and pushed carts, or carried sacks full of all their worldly possessions on their backs. Often the sacks were so large that one could not see its carrier.

Germans stood ready at the entrances to the apartment buildings, shooting anyone leaving after the fifteen minutes had expired. There were no questions and no exceptions.

Teddy and Simcha started pulling the sleds through the snow-covered street. The snow made the ground slippery underneath them and made it difficult to pull the sled. Every step was a struggle for Teddy until they were finally able to build some momentum.

"Anka!" Esther screamed at the top of her lungs, pointing to the fourth floor of the apartment.

"Are you kidding me?" cried Pola.

"Keep moving," Touba told everyone.

Teddy threw the sled straps down and took off in a full sprint towards the apartment.

"Get back here, Tanchum!" Simcha yelled.

No Germans were standing outside of the building and Teddy figured he had two minutes until he was out of time. He took the stairs three at a time, as he had done so many times in the past, and entered the apartment. He searched every room desperately trying to find Anka.

He was about to give up when he found the doll. She was sitting next to the kitchen sink, probably from Esther watching Touba pack her pots and pans.

Teddy grabbed the doll and bolted down the stairs, jumping the final four steps of each staircase. He flew through the front door, where three Germans stood pointing their guns at him. Teddy covered his face, waiting for the shot, but nothing happened. He was still under the time limit. He had taken two steps towards his family when the Germans opened fire.

He felt his spine twist and muscles spasm from the power and proximity of the weapon blasts. Teddy's heart raced and his adrenaline skyrocketed. He turned around to find the ice cream shop owner lying dead. It was almost as if he was sitting upright against the door. His eyes stared lifelessly into the distance. Fresh drops of ice cream covered his beard from preparing the day's supply.

Teddy caught up to his family. Simcha slapped his face then hugged him. Knowing he deserved it, Teddy did not say anything and hugged his father tightly. He turned to Esther, handing her Anka.

"This doll will be the end of me," remarked Teddy as Esther thanked him.

They continued to walk north towards Baluty. Sheer panic and fear spread through the streets of Lodz. Once the soldiers had shot anyone leaving their buildings after the allotted time, they went inside and searched for stragglers. Endless gunshots echoed from building interiors. Soldiers found and killed people hiding in piano boxes, under floorboards, in closets and desks. Muzzle flashes lit up windows.

Snipers climbed to rooftops and randomly fired at people in the slow-moving herd. As more and more people fell victim to the sniper fire, the crowd picked up its pace.

A man pushing a cart loaded with his wife, two children and their belongings took a bullet to the head. Blood sprayed all over his family as he fell to the street. Before they started screaming, a stranger came over and pushed their cart forward, aware of what the family's fate would be if they stayed behind. The family never said goodbye to their husband and father but watched him vanish in the distance under the feet of thousands of people.

A mother held her infant in one arm and her daughter's hand with the other while her husband pulled their sled. The daughter bent over to pick up a toy and became the victim of a sniper. Her six-year-old hand went limp in her mother's grasp. Knowing they could not stop, but unwilling to leave their little girl behind, the father placed her on the sled and pulled her towards Baluty.

Dead bodies covered the road. Blood from their fatal wounds changed the pure white snow to a dark red. Pola jumped at every shot heard and looked back continuously to ensure her family was still intact.

The family entered the dilapidated section of Baluty with no idea where to go or what to do. People were searching the crumbling buildings looking for places to stay. The family travelled up Zachodnia Street, making a left onto Lutomierska Street, simply following a group of people in front of them. The crowd of travelling Jews eventually thinned out. They turned onto Gnieznienska Street and started looking for somewhere to live.

They found an apartment on the first floor of a four-story building. It consisted of one bedroom and a kitchen and was the only room available in the building. The apartment complex was filled to the brim with people. Two and three-bedroom apartments housed more families than one thought possible and people had trouble moving around. The residence they found was miniscule but at least they would stay together and have some little sense of privacy.

Teddy started to unload the sleds. Shots continued in the distance. He shook his head in disgust at what he witnessed. Inside the apartment, Esther kissed Anka and vowed never to let her out of her sight again. Touba consoled Pola, who had trouble comprehending what had happened, and Simcha went around to the other apartments in the building to introduce himself and get a better feel for the situation.

Teddy had begun unloading the second sled when someone tapped his shoulder. To his surprise, Chaim was standing behind him. Teddy had not seen him in a few weeks. Chaim's family had gone into hiding when the round-ups intensified. The two boys hugged each other, happy they had both survived the day's events.

Standing next to Chaim was a boy named Asher. He was the same age as Teddy and Chaim, but had grown up in the southern part of Lodz. He had the same mischievous personality as Teddy – he loved to push limits to find out just how far he could go.

"Where did you guys end up?" asked Teddy.

"We're right up the road here on Gnieznienska," Chaim answered.

Chaim's family was one of the first to move into Baluty when the announcement came. They ended up on Gnieznienska Street because it was on the far end of the area considered "contaminated" and figured they would be away from trouble. They found a big three-bedroom apartment, thinking it would only be for them. To their surprise, a few weeks later, two more families moved into the place. Each family had one bedroom, Asher's being one of them.

The boys helped Teddy unload the sled and were envious that his family had the apartment to themselves. They agreed to meet up in the next few days after things settled.

For the rest of the day, the family unloaded the sleds and organized their new home. They all hoped it would be a temporary stay and they would be back in their home, although they knew the reality was likely the opposite. They had no choice but to wait and hope for the best.

That night Touba made dinner for her family. It did not take long for the tiny apartment to smell like fried onions. Not knowing how long they would live in Baluty, she had packed up their entire pantry and thrown it on the sled.

"No wonder the sled was so heavy," Simcha joked.

The children laughed as Touba shot him an evil look, eventually smiling. No one said much around the dinner table that night. Everyone sat quietly, thinking about the day's events and what the future held.

Lights over the table flickered constantly, casting eerie shadows on the walls. Even when the lights stayed on, they only let off a dim glow, making it difficult to see. Esther constantly shifted on the uncomfortable wooden chair. Anxiety overtook Pola. She did not recognize the strange noises around the apartment building. The apartment was a far cry from the comfortable home they had fled.

Baluty, though not far away from where they had lived, appeared to be an entirely different city. Old, worn-down cobblestone streets lay between rows of buildings in serious disarray. Paint peeled from their exteriors. It was impossible to walk down the street and find a building that did not have at least three broken windows. Overgrown trees and grass gave the appearance of a deserted city. However, that was no longer the case as now families of five shared one-bedroom apartments. .

The dilapidated exteriors were nothing compared to the conditions inside. The smell of dirt and mold could nearly choke anyone who entered. Paint peeled on every wall. Floorboards creaked and groaned, screaming for the person to move off quickly. Community bathrooms on each floor were filthy. Most porcelain sinks were broken and almost none of them had running water. The toilets were even worse – if that were possible. If a toilet actually did have any water, it was minimal, never allowing for the proper disposal of waste. Electricity was all but non-existent.

"How can people live like this?" Pola asked.

"You do the best with what you've been given," answered Touba.

Everyone had a restless night. No one was used to sleeping in such a confined space. Simcha and Touba shared the full-sized bed with Esther while Teddy and Pola slept on the floor. Their beds were layers of thin blankets. The sink faucet dripped continuously and seemed to get louder as the night went on.

Esther suffered from continual nightmares as her young brain tried to process everything she had experienced in the previous months. She mumbled words in her sleep and shifted from side to side, occasionally kicking Touba. Simcha lay on his side, staring out the window. He knew the gravity of his family's situation and tried to think of a way out. He wondered if they would have had a better chance fleeing Lodz with their neighbors or if the gamble to stay would eventually pay off.

The next morning, the girls cleaned the apartment with limited supplies while Touba emphasized how living with dignity could help brighten their circumstances.

Simcha and Teddy walked around the apartment introducing themselves to their new neighbors. The apartment building had twenty-five individual apartments that comfortably accommodated ninety people. Teddy counted one hundred ninety-eight people in the apartment. The most crowded residence was a three-bedroom apartment on the fourth floor. Seventeen people lived there.

"And you thought we didn't have enough space!" Simcha joked.

On the second floor, they met Chaim Kwart, who lived with his wife Anna, mother-in-law Sala, and sister-in-law Rebekah. They shared a two-bedroom apartment with a family of four. He was a tall man in his mid-twenties and in great shape. He was a technician who worked a lot on plumbing, attributing his health to the physical work he performed.

Even though Kwart liked his line of work, he wanted to become a baker. He was saving money to open his own bakery and had almost saved up enough to move forward when Germany invaded.

"You would get along beautifully with my wife," said Simcha.

Kwart and Simcha hit it off immediately. They had similar personalities and wanted to do right by their families. They did not know what to make of their current situation but knew they had to make the best of it.

As Kwart and Simcha talked, Teddy went in search of his Chaim. Not knowing where to begin looking, Teddy walked up Gnieznienska Street calling out his friend's name. It did not take long before Chaim came huffing and puffing out of his apartment, three buildings down.

Laughing, Teddy asked, "How many cookies did you eat today?" in German, imitating the soldier who had kicked Chaim's stomach. Chaim answered with an angry stare, which lasted six seconds until he could not hold back his laughter any longer. He wrapped his arm around Teddy's shoulders, rubbing his knuckles over Teddy's scalp until he begged him to stop.

"Come, let's explore," said Chaim.

They started walking away when the sound of running footsteps caught their attention. Before Teddy could turn, a strong pressure pushed down on both of his shoulders. Asher jumped over him effortlessly.

"You guys aren't leaving without me, are you?" he asked.

"Of course not," Chaim answered.

The boys walked around their new neighborhood, trying to see where they might fit in. The further they walked into their "designated area", the more populated the cobblestone streets became. A man set up shop in front of his apartment building and sold ties. Another man was selling shoes further up the road. A few older kids hung out on the stairs of a building that looked like it would collapse any minute.

Snow that fell days earlier was now a muddy, splashing slush. Some puddles were so deep and wide, a person had to cross the street to get around them. Avoiding the puddles, the boys walked further into Baluty but it finally became impossible to continue.

They turned around and began heading home. Asher tripped on a stone sticking out a few inches higher than those around it and fell to the ground. He landed in a puddle, sending a wave of slushy mess toward Teddy and Chaim.

"My mother is going to beat my ass!" exclaimed Chaim.

Teddy reached down to help Asher up as they laughed but it became apparent that Asher had sprained his ankle badly and was not able to put his full weight on it. He rose to his feet, putting his arms around Teddy and Chaim's shoulders. Slowly, he took a few steps, easing into each one.

The boys took their time getting home. Turning on Gnieznienska Street, the boys never thought the crappy road looked so good.

"Thanks, Tanchum," said Asher.

Before Teddy could respond, a ball of packed slush hit Chaim in the back of his head and exploded on impact. Pieces of ice flew everywhere. Chaim, shocked by the blow, lost his footing and fell to the floor. At the same time, Asher stepped on his bad ankle. He let out a painful cry and fell on top of Chaim.

Teddy stood alone and did not have time to figure out what happened before an ice ball struck his shoulder. The painful throbbing was immediate. He looked to his right to find four teenagers heading in his direction.

"Fall down, you stupid Jew," jeered one of the boys, bending over to pick up more slush.

Another ball of ice hit Teddy in his right hip followed by one to the stomach. As the young Poles approached, Teddy's heart began to race. His pupils dilated as he clenched both fists, preparing himself for the inevitable fact he was about to be beaten. Teddy was not going to go down without a fight.

The ringleader came within arm's length of Teddy and wound back to strike. Teddy raised his arms to protect himself from a blow to his face. The teen's fist began its forward motion when he received a blow of his own.

The icy slush ball struck the teenager's temple, catching him completely off guard. He stumbled to the ground, landing on Asher's ankle and causing him to let out an agonizing scream. The other teenagers, not expecting this turn of events, stopped in their tracks.

"Why don't you pick a fair fight?" called a Jewish teenager who was standing by the building that looked like it was collapsing. Four other teenagers stood around him. The group of boys approached the troublemaking *goyim*.

The teen lying on the street, seeing that he would not likely win this fight, jumped up quickly. He looked at his friends who were waiting for his command and motioned with his head for the group to leave.

"Filthy horned Jews, you'll get what you deserve," snarled the deflated teen as he walked away with his posse.

"Thanks for your help," said Teddy, turning to face his rescuers. "I could have taken them," he added with a smile.

"Sure you could have," the teen grinned back. "Those pieces of *drek* have been terrorizing the street all day," he continued. "Finally got what was coming to them."

"Well, I think you made that one guy *plotz*!" said Teddy.

The group of teens laughed and assisted Chaim and Asher to their feet. They helped Asher to his apartment. Though his ankle was swollen it could bear some weight. Everyone parted ways for the night.

When Teddy arrived home, the apartment was crammed with people. Chuh Chuh Rose and Cila were over, as were Kwart, Anna, Sala and Rebekah. Simcha had convinced Kwart to come for the Sabbath, performed in secret as its observance had been banned by the Nazis months ago.

Simcha placed a blanket over the window to block the candlelight. As was customary, Touba lit the candles and recited the prayers to bring in the Sabbath. She then placed the lit candles in the corner furthest away from the window to minimize the chances of candlelight escaping.

The adults sat around the table while the children sat on the floor. As they prepared to eat, yelling erupted outside. What started out as an argument soon turned to screams for help. Unable to go outside as a result of the curfew and unwilling to risk moving the blanket, all they could do was sit and listen.

"Get away from my family," screamed a man. "Help! Somebody!"

Harsh anti-Semitic responses answered his pleas for assistance.

"Get out of my home, you filthy Jew. You have no right to be here."

"Please, stop, leave us alone," a woman shouted.

A skirmish followed. Unable to see the fight left everyone to his or her own imagination. Sounds of rocks hitting brick walls and breaking glass cut through the otherwise silent night. The numbers were not in favor of the Jews who occupied the Pole's former residence. Two additional voices cheered on the fight, announcing it like a boxing match.

There was a loud thud, then silence.

"His Jewish face hurt my hand," said a voice, followed by laughter. "Come it's getting late. Let's go home."

Footsteps began to walk away, leaving a woman to cry by her husband.

"Mom, is Dad ok?" a little boy asked.

"Yes, my beautiful boy, now go inside," his mother answered.

The rest of the night was silent.

The Znamirowski family stayed in the apartment after that night. Daily round-ups for forced labor became more intense, and Poles and Germans alike frequented the streets of Baluty, free to mug people, vandalize buildings and rob apartments.

By the end of April, the Germans completed erecting a barbed wire and wooden fence around the area designated as the Jewish ghetto, secluding the Jews from the rest of the city. Gnieznienska Street was at a far end of the ghetto and surrounded by barbed wire on its west and northern sides.

German police constantly patrolled the fence to ensure no Jews escaped or had contact with the outside world. Touba and Simcha had mixed emotions about its closing. Touba was sure the Germans had segregated them for a reason and, based on how things had gone since the occupation, it could not be good. Simcha, on the other hand, was glad the Germans and Poles could no longer gain access to them and they were safe from further unnecessary torment.

After officially closing the ghetto to the outside world, the Jews trapped inside felt an overall peace. They were finally free to roam around without the fears that had been plaguing them for months, but the reality was that their troubles were only beginning.

#

8: Better In Or Out?

It soon became apparent that everyone was dependent on the Germans for anything from outside the barbed wire fences. Farmland did not exist inside the ghetto. The delivery of food and medicine became top priority.

The Germans had appointed Chaim Mordechai Rumkowski head of the *Altestenrat* – Council of Elders – before the ghetto was sealed. He became responsible for maintaining order and, over time, forming an organized city within the ghetto.

Circumstances deteriorated more rapidly than anticipated and extreme overpopulation was just the tip of the iceberg. Hopes of improved living conditions stayed alive in everyone, but days turned to weeks and weeks to months. There appeared to be no limit to how appalling life inside the barbed wire could be.

Most buildings had no plumbing or running water. People relieved themselves in buckets and emptied them on the streets. The lack of sanitation quickly led to widespread disease.

People had long since eaten the food they had brought with them. Extreme hunger became problematic as Rumkowski's system began.

Simcha's distrust in Lodz's banks paid off. He had always maintained a careful watch and accounting of his money and kept it on hand. This turned out to be an advantage over other Jews who had money in banks they could no longer visit.

A market place opened not too far from the Znamirowski apartment. Occasionally, Teddy and Simcha walked by to meet people and see what was going on in different areas of the ghetto. Not wanting to bring attention to his money, Simcha never bought anything.

Whatever a person needed was at the market. Traders sold shoes, ties, books, and furniture to earn money to purchase food. Teddy walked up and down the streets looking at different vendors lining the road. He noticed the prices of items and began to scheme about how to make extra money on his own.

At the beginning of the summer, Rumki, named after Rumkowski, became the official currency of the ghetto. Outside the fence it held no value, but inside it bought almost anything. People lined the streets of Marysinska to exchange their cash for Rumkis. Those who did not have money sold jewelry and other valuables.

Productivity became the only way to sustain survival in the ghetto. Food rations were a meager loaf of bread, a few vegetables and some brown water that was supposed to pass as coffee. The rations were meant to last for five days but most people finished them in two or three. If a person worked, they received a bowl of soup at lunchtime consisting of hot water and a few floating barley beans.

Pola, Teddy, Esther, Cila, Chaim and Asher went to school during the day. It provided a sense of normalcy and stability in their lives. Teddy had hated school in his former life and found it too easy for his liking, but now he looked forward to it.

At school with other children, he was a child again. A full curriculum of science, history, language and writing took on new meaning for him, replacing the nightmares in his head with imagination and wonder.

At lunchtime, children received the soup they'd hungered for all morning. Impatiently, they stood in line with metal soup bowls, waiting for the precious life-sustaining liquid and devoured it in seconds. To start with, Teddy tried to be first in line to spend less time waiting. Within days, however, he learned that the children at the front of the line received watered-down soup, so if he waited until towards the end, there was a better chance of soup with more substance. More substance equaled a better chance of survival.

Esther and Cila were in the same classroom. The hunger overtaking the ghetto affected her class more than the older kids and it showed in the energy level of the children. Most put their heads down and slept, unable to focus on what was going on around them.

Esther and Cila, however, enjoyed school and saw it as a world away from their hard one at home. The class danced and sang songs. Anka became a main attraction as Esther told stories about Tanchum saving her repeatedly.

Compared to her siblings, Pola had a harder time losing herself in schoolwork. She caught herself staring out the window from time to time, disgusted at the conditions she saw. Filth covered roads and sidewalks. Feces and urine always found their way onto the paths people walked. Once in love with school, she now attended only to receive her soup.

Beggars lined the streets on the way to school. They asked for nothing specific, always hoping for anything but, unfortunately, the children had nothing to give.

Simcha worked in a factory making army boots for the Germans. His responsibility was cutting out soles for the boots. The factory was overcrowded and people climbed over one another to get to different workstations.

Touba and Kwart's wife, Anna, worked in a textile factory sewing pants for the German army. Conversations were the same, no matter where a person worked. People talked about the good old days when food was plentiful and clean sheets were an everyday experience.

Kwart became a police officer and security guard for a judge. Gnieznienska Street was also where the court, public prosecutor's office and investigators' offices were located. Kwart's job was seen as more important than most, and, as such, he received a larger portion of soup and bread. Kwart promised to share his relative good fortune with Simcha when he could.

Over the next few months, living conditions in the ghetto worsened. Rations that barely kept people through five days were now allocated only every eight days by the Nazis. Everyone was on the brink of starvation. The number of dead on the streets increased dramatically. Typhus and tuberculosis were rampant throughout the ghetto.

On the walk to school one day, Asher didn't seem like himself.

"I don't feel good," he complained.

He knew staying home from school meant missing lunchtime soup and that was something his thinning body could not handle.

After eating his soup, Asher left to head home.

"Do you want me to go with you?" Teddy asked.

"No, I'll be fine," Asher answered.

He sluggishly walked through the front door and eventually out of sight.

At the end of the day, the children met up to walk home.

"Where's Asher?" Cila asked.

"He went home after eating," Chaim answered.

"He looked really pale today," Pola, added.

As they approached Gnieznienska Street, Chaim separated, heading into his apartment as the Znamirowskis continued towards theirs. Chuh Chuh Rose waited for them while Touba cooked a potato and rutabaga in water, making a soup of her own.

Simcha came home half an hour later, equally exhausted from the twelve-hour workday and lack of nourishment. He took off his coat and laid it on one of the kitchen chairs. Quietly he sat down in a chair, staring off into space, thinking about the changes their lives had witnessed over the last year and a half.

His hands used to be soft from only gripping paintbrush handles. Now they were rough and blistered from pressing and cutting shoe soles. His smooth face showed signs of aging from the physical hardships challenging him daily.

The soup did not last long. Esther finished her bowl before Chuh Chuh Rose even received hers. No one talked at the table anymore, as everyone was too busy finishing their soup. After dinner, they went to bed early to conserve energy for the following day's labor.

The next morning Chaim met Teddy outside before walking to school.

"Asher didn't come home yesterday," said Chaim.

"What do you mean?" asked Teddy.

"No one knows where he is," continued Chaim. "We're all worried about him."

"Where could he have gone?" Teddy asked.

Chaim shrugged his shoulders, not having any answers to give Teddy. Pola, Esther and Cila joined them walking to school.

The group approached Lutomierska Street, about to make a left, when a feral cat caught Esther's interest. She watched the cat run off towards the right before letting out an ear-curdling scream.

Gaining the attention of the children around her, Esther pointed to the barbed wire fence. A lifeless body was latched onto it, his coat caught on the barbs. The dead person did not surprise anyone. They had seen the sight before. The Germans had issued a warning to the Jews when first enclosing the ghetto: they would shoot anyone thought to be leaving.

Nearing the body, the facial features became eerily familiar. Refusing to believe what he saw, Chaim mumbled "no" repeatedly. Teddy leaned in to confirm the identity. He looked at his friend and family and said, "It's him."

Asher had been dead for a while, his body frozen in time at the moment of his murder. His left hand gripped tightly onto the fence while his right arm hung lifelessly by his side. His torso tilted backward. The barbs had grabbed a hold of his coat and had refused to let go through the night. His head leaned back, making his eyes gaze endlessly at the grey sky.

While staring at the dead boy, questioning his stupidity to go near the fence, Teddy noticed a calm, peaceful expression on Asher's face. He was free from his painful life. Pola turned and ran to find help. She bumped into Kwart walking to work and explained what they'd found. The children did not want to take Asher off the fence for fear they would meet the same fate.

Kwart arrived with another officer and removed Asher from the fence's grasp. Laying him on the ground exposed the bullet hole in his chest but no one could answer the question as to why he had gone to the fence in the first place.

It was a quiet walk to school that morning. Everyone thought the same thing but nobody spoke about it. No one had seen it coming. Teddy could not get Asher's expression out of his head. The peaceful look haunted him more than the situation itself.

The children were almost to school when a cart loaded with loaves of bread passed in front of them. Horses never pulled carts anymore. Two Jewish boys grabbing a hold of horse harnesses struggled to pull the cart forward, while two more boys pushed from behind. Cobblestone streets made the ride rough and every once in a while an outlying stone stopped the cart in its tracks, painfully yanking back the boys pulling it. Progress was slow but they managed.

The strong smells were powerful enough to levitate the starving children off the ground. Smiles grew wide on their faces but painful hunger in their stomachs brought them down to reality. Two boys across the street could not resist their hunger any longer. They darted for the cart and grabbed some loaves of bread before running off. They did not make it far. Members of the Jewish police escorted bread deliveries.

The police officers threw the teenagers to the ground, kicking and punching them violently. Passers-by ignored the boys' pleas for help and apologies, continuing with their own struggles. The sight of Jews fighting Jews did not sit right with Teddy. *Now we fight ourselves*, he thought.

Eventually, the police dragged the two misfits off the road and out of sight, leaving their blood and screams behind.

#

9: Ghetto Life

Seasons had turned. Green leaves sprouted, changed colors and died off. Snow had fallen and melted away, but the terrible conditions remained. Meager rations caused severe hunger and increased numbers succumbed to starvation. Strong feelings of helplessness and wasting away had overtaken the ghetto.

Garbage, filth, feces, death and disease lined the streets. People slowly trudged through muddy cobblestone roads as unrecognizable shells of their former selves. Dirt covered once-beautiful faces. Knots replaced long flowing hair. Outbreaks of lice occurred everywhere. Pressed clothes became raggedy. Bright eyes turned dull.

The Znamirowskis felt the full weight of ghetto life. Simcha's cash – traded in for Rumkis – was all but gone. On occasion, the family made trips to 7 Ciesielska Street to the "Bank for the Purchase of Valuable Objects and Clothing" to sell their fur coats and jewelry in exchange for Rumkis. They no longer owned items holding any value in the ghetto which made them completely dependent on the system for survival. They needed another way to make money and get food.

Rumors spread of spies searching for illegal activities taking place. A real fear developed about the Gestapo having eyes everywhere. Friends and families developed a strong distrust of one another. The terrible situations people faced daily turned them into rats, jumping at opportunities to tell on each other if it meant a little more food or better chances for survival.

At the factory, Simcha overheard a conversation between some of his fellow workers. One mentioned he heard a newsflash about events occurring on a few of the fronts. Amused by what he said, the men listened intently with widened eyes of hope.

Three days later, the man telling the stories had disappeared. Theories developed about the Gestapo finding out and taking him to the *kripo* better known as the *Rote Haus* – Red House. The red bricks making up its exterior came to represent the building's purpose: torture. The building itself gave onlookers a sense of fear and evil.

The *kripo* was originally the parish house for St. Mary's Assumption Church located on Koscielna Street. It was transformed into a police station when Baluty became the ghetto. Few people who entered the Red House left alive.

There were stories about the basement being a dungeon where inconceivable torture took place to gather information on both legal and illegal activities within the ghetto walls. Even if someone did not have useful information for the Gestapo, he or she had little chance of leaving the *kripo* alive.

The fact no one knew who turned the man in made everyone a suspect. Anyone participating in illegal activities knew not to share this fact with anyone for fear of ending up at the Red House.

At the beginning of fall, 1941, the Znamirowskis sat with Kwart and his family to eat soup Touba had made by combining everyone's rations for dinner. Kwart had terrible news: the Germans planned to transport twenty thousand western European Jews into the ghetto.

"Where will they stay?" Touba asked, frustrated. "We barely have enough room for ourselves."

She put her head into her hands and started sobbing. Simcha put his arms around her, trying to console her.

"We'll be ok," he said. "We've made it this far. We can keep going."

"As long as they don't cut our rations, things should stay the same," said Kwart, offering words of encouragement.

A month later, Teddy and Chaim were playing in the street with a ball they'd found a few weeks prior while walking home from school. Esther and Cila played with Anka as usual, and Pola sat next to a school friend.

Two children not more than six years old picked through garbage across the street, searching for anything edible. It was a punishable offense to do this but nobody in the immediate area was going to stop them.

"Hey Tanchum, come see," said Chaim, pointing down the street.

Teddy's eyes looked up to see where his friend's finger pointed. In the distance, a caravan of people walked in their direction. It reminded Teddy of the day his family had first entered Baluty.

The people walked towards them with horse-pulled carts and sleds loaded with belongings. The Nazis had transported them to Lodz from all over Western Europe, but mainly Germany. As the caravan containing thousands of people walked past the children, both sides could not believe what they saw.

The newcomers were dressed in their best clothes. They were clean-shaven, washed and healthy.

"They're not going to last long here," said a thinner Chaim.

Faces of disgust met the children as the outsiders walked by. To them, the ghetto was the definition of a slum. The children wore raggedy clothes covered in filth. They appeared unhealthily thin and hardened by the atmosphere around them. The buildings and streets had accumulated dirt and the smell of the area was nauseating. Based on the ghetto's current state, it would not take long for the newcomers to blend in or perish.

Kwart was right: the addition of twenty thousand Jews did not have an effect on the already terrible conditions they lived under.

A few weeks later, the children received devastating news. The Germans were closing the schools down. No schools meant no lunchtime soup, which posed a huge threat to the children's health. Soup was equivalent to life and worth its weight in gold. Without it, chances of survival diminished greatly.

Teddy and Pola joined the ghetto workforce to receive their soup. Pola found a job in a textile factory sewing women's underwear and dresses. The women who'd worked there for a while were standoffish at first, not wanting anything to do with the "new girl", but Pola was a hard worker and quickly earned the respect of her fellow workers.

Teddy and Chaim found employment at a factory producing wooden toys for German children. Children became the workforce after the schools closed down. Teddy's personality made him popular with other children in the factory and his strong work ethic gained favor with the supervisor. Chaim stuck close to Teddy, making good off the connections his friend created.

Touba would not allow Esther to work in the factories. She feared they were too dangerous for a little girl, but this meant Esther would not receive any soup. The family decided to rotate days and each gave Esther half of their soup to help maintain her health and strength.

Hunger was constant. If a person was not eating, they were thinking about the next time they would be. For most, it might be a few days. The powerful effects of malnourishment blocked rational thought and many people could not restrain themselves and eat moderately when they had the chance. People hid edible items at all times to ensure they were not stolen by neighbors, friends and family alike.

Cila worked with Chuh Chuh Rose in a furniture factory constructing wooden bed frames and posts. The supervisor was extremely strict and did not hesitate to withhold soup from workers if production numbers were not up to par. Par was whatever he saw fit. It took two days of no soup and figuring out the system before Cila became an expert in woodwork.

One day at the toy factory, Teddy overheard his supervisor talking to a man about his wife who had come down with pneumonia but did not want to go to the hospital. Teddy knew a nurse who lived in his apartment building and thought he could benefit from this situation.

He approached the nurse after work and bargained with her for antibiotics. They came to the agreement that Teddy would give her half his soup ration in return for medicine. Teddy was also responsible for smuggling it out of the hospital. Food was the most sought-after commodity with the strongest bargaining power. Both he and the nurse knew the horror stories about the Red House and agreed it was best if they kept their operation as quiet as possible. Other people would not hesitate to turn them in to the Gestapo if it meant receiving food in return.

Teddy walked into the hospital the next day and headed up a flight of stairs to the second floor. The wing was crowded with sick people suffering from all types of ailments. The beds, lined up with head posts against the walls, created a center aisle where doctors and nurses walked, monitoring their patients.

People coughed all around Teddy. To the left was a wing full of patients suffering from tuberculosis. To the right were those with typhus. Straight ahead was a general wing for influenza and extreme malnutrition. Patients occupied every bed. Teddy walked through the center aisle of the miscellaneous wing trying to ignore the cries for help. Eventually, he found his friend standing by a desk documenting medical information.

She looked up, noticing that someone was approaching her. Seeing it was Teddy, she blinked twice and touched her right shoulder, signifying she'd stashed the medicine in a garbage can by the stairs. If she'd scratched her head, that would have meant no medicine was available.

Teddy walked to the garbage can and looked inside, but, much to his dismay, it was empty. He turned to the nurse but she was no longer standing at the desk. He peered inside one more time and still saw nothing. Becoming flustered, Teddy turned and headed towards the stairs, but then it hit him. Stopping short in his tracks, he spun around, returning to the garbage can. He tilted it back, looking at the floor, and was relieved at what he found. Packaged neatly was the medicine he needed. Cautiously, he looked about, bending down to pick up the antibiotics before running downstairs and out of the building.

The next day, Teddy went up to his supervisor, telling him he would be able to get antibiotics for his wife.

"How can you do that? You're just a child," said the supervisor.

"I'll have them for you, guaranteed," answered Teddy.

"What's this going to cost me?" his supervisor asked.

"Well, what are you willing to pay?" said Teddy.

"An extra half bowl of soup a day for a week," his supervisor responded.

"Deal," said Teddy.

Teddy broke even between the nurse and his supervisor, giving a half bowl of soup to the nurse to get half a bowl back from the supervisor, but his ultimate gain was having the supervisor as a contact.

In the weeks that followed, ghetto inhabitants utilized Teddy's services for themselves or loved ones without having to check into the hospital, sacrificing half bowls of soup in return. Teddy brought his extra soup home in a small tin pitcher he'd found, making sure to share it with his family rather than keep it all for himself. The soup wasn't a lot, especially divided five ways, but it was more than most received and made sacrificing a half bowl of soup for Esther less painful on the mind and body.

Two months into his operation, Teddy ran up the stairs of the hospital, walking his familiar path through the miscellaneous wing only to find the nurse was not there.

But she's always here, Teddy thought.

He searched the tuberculosis wing, then the typhus wing but could not find her anywhere. He walked up to one of the physicians, gently pulling his coat.

"Excuse me sir, do you know where Mrs. Minski is?" asked Teddy.

The physician looked over his shoulder to see who was speaking. Seeing a young boy, he lowered his guard.

"Who is asking?" the physician replied.

"My name is Tanchum, I'm her neighbor," answered Teddy. Thinking fast, he lifted his tin pitcher pretending it was hers. "She forgot her soup bowl."

"She was taken away this morning," the doctor answered.

"Taken away?" Teddy questioned.

"Gestapo," said the physician.

Teddy turned quickly. His face had frozen, and his eyes were as wide open as his mouth.

They've found me, he thought.

#

10: One By One

The physician did not need to say more. Teddy's heart dropped to the floor. *How did they find out?* he asked himself. Panicked, he ran out of the hospital. The whole way home, he looked over his shoulder, fearful of someone following him.

Are they after me? Teddy thought. *Did she tell them about me? Of course she did. Why wouldn't she?*

Thoughts of the Red House raced through his mind. Finally home, he was relieved to see no Gestapo waiting, at least not yet.

Teddy was jumpy at dinner. Every sound outside lifted him off his chair. When the knock on the door came, he almost fainted. The pounding of his heart felt like it was exploding out of his chest.

When Kwart entered, Teddy was so relieved he ran up and kissed him.

"Did you hear about Hana Minski?" Kwart asked.

"No, what about her?" Simcha answered.

"Taken by the Gestapo," said Kwart. "I don't know why."

Simcha and the family knew what Teddy was up to with Hana but had never told anybody. The risk was too great. They continued playing the innocent card, not knowing who could be listening.

Later that night, Teddy had a nightmare. He was running from Jewish police officers for an unknown reason. Continuing to evade them, he ended up in the middle of Baluty market. He walked the endless rows of merchants selling off their personal belongings. Their clothes were too big for them. One of the peddlers took off his shirt and sold it.

Teddy was horrified at the merchant's condition, which was almost entirely skin and bones. He thought it was impossible for someone to be alive in that state. He ran, eventually ending up at the foot of a food mountain. *Perogies, golabki, babkas* were endless. The smell knocked Teddy off his feet.

As he lay there, he stared at the endless supply of food in front of him. He stood back up, then grabbed a few *perogies* and ate them quickly before someone else came along to take them. He piled *babka* into his mouth until he was unable to chew.

Teddy filled his pockets with *khruchikis* cookies. He tucked his shirt into his pants and stuffed it with *perogies* and *golabki*.

My family is going to love this, he thought.

The sense of joy did not last long. The mountain of food began melting into the cobblestone street. He reached into his pocket for a cookie but it had gone. The *golabki* in his shirt vanished too.

"No!" Teddy screamed at the top of his lungs.

A woman's scream answered his. Teddy's gaze lifted upward from the street to the building in front of him.

The sky grew dark. Heavy clouds formed overhead. A single light shone onto the building and Teddy recognized what he was looking at. The red brick was undeniable proof. He heard another shriek inside the building and realized he knew from whom those screams were coming.

He turned to run home. The further he ran from the Red House, the louder the screams became. By the time he had reached home the screams were deafening.

#

Pola took her pillow and hit Teddy. He woke up screaming, covered in sweat, but relieved it was just a dream.

The Gestapo never came for Teddy. Hana kept her promise. She never told anyone about the operation.

Teddy struggled with guilt over Hana's fate. If Teddy had not approached her she would still be alive. The promise of more food drove people to extreme measures, despite the consequences.

November came quickly and so did the cold. Dworska Street became the most popular place in the ghetto. The Coal Department was located there in a dilapidated one-story wooden building. People lined the roads to pick up their ration of coal, which was not enough to heat anything.

Having sold their fur coats and heavier clothing for Rumkis, the Znamirowskis did not have proper attire to survive the dropping temperatures. The temperatures were so cold they only left the apartment to work.

Conditions in factories became more horrific and demanding as time went on. With no energy from lack of nourishment and the high demand to produce quality products for Germans, the Nazis forced the Jews to pull off the impossible. The two consolations to working were heated rooms in factories and hot soup, which grew thinner each month.

Teddy and Pola climbed the wooden stairs of the bridge crossing Zgierska Street. A woman, ten people ahead of them, stopped in her tracks. She turned, took off her coat and handed it to a young girl standing behind her. She smiled at everyone in front and behind her. She then looked up at the sky before placing her two frozen hands on the handrail of the bridge. Slowly, she looked down Zgierska Street, peering over the ghetto border at the only glimpse of "normal" life she had seen in years.

The woman placed her left leg on a piece of wood siding. She stepped up to the next plank with her right leg. With one final look at the sky, the woman threw herself off the bridge.

Four bullets met her as she landed on her feet seven meters below. The woman fell backwards onto the street and did not move.

Traffic on the bridge picked up again as if nothing had happened. The commuters were indifferent to death, seeing it every day. Everyone kept their eyes straight, fearing the consequences of being caught looking down at the body.

Pola shivered uncontrollably. Her thin, single-layer jacket was no match for the 20-degree weather. She wanted to run to work for warmth but had no energy to make the attempt and did not want to bring attention to herself.

Teddy grabbed her trembling hands and used his own to warm them. Pola appreciated his effort, even though it did not help much. She thanked him with a slight smile. Arriving at Pola's factory, Teddy saw her inside before heading to work himself.

When they got home later, Chuh Chuh Rose sat at the table with Esther. It was Pola's day to bring home half her soup for Esther. Teddy, seeing Pola's condition, brought home half of his as well, allowing Pola to have a little extra at dinner.

Chuh Chuh Rose sobbed uncontrollably. She was a shadow of her former self. The woman who always dressed up to the nines now wore rags. She had tied her hair into a pathetic form of a ponytail with a piece of string found on the street. Her nails were dirty and her skin rough from hard labor. Life in the ghetto had taken over.

Simcha and Touba walked through the door together, having met prior to crossing over the bridge. Seeing Rose so distraught, Touba told the children to go to Kwart's apartment.

Pola and Esther went upstairs to Kwart and Anna while Teddy stayed behind. Quietly, he placed his frostbitten ear to the door, listening to the conversation inside.

Rose could not pull herself together and was difficult to understand as she broke down crying between every sentence.

"Cila," she said.

"What happened to Cila?" Simcha asked.

"Cila," she sobbed again, unable to put into words what she had seen.

Touba walked around the table and pulled up a chair to sit next to Rose. Leaning in closely, she asked, "Rose, what happened?"

#

Cila had started to cry when the supervisor yelled at her for not working fast enough. As punishment, he docked her lunchtime soup and remained on her case for the rest of the day.

Not understanding why the supervisor as picking on her, Cila decided to watch her progress compared to everyone else. She worked twice as fast. Bronia, a young girl with fiery red curly hair, told her not to take it personally.

"He picks on someone new every day, docking their soup so he doubles his," she told Cila. "He's greedy and enjoys watching others suffer."

"Why doesn't someone say something?" asked Cila.

Bronia shrugged her shoulders. "Who knows what the punishment would be then," she answered.

At lunchtime, Bronia gave Cila a few swallows of her own soup to help keep overwhelming hunger at bay – a feeling she knew well.

Rose and Cila walked home shivering in the brutal cold, the snow on the ground making the streets impassable.

Cila held onto Rose. The warmth from their hands was the only thing reminding them they were alive. Everything was a gloomy shade of grey. Poverty and death was all around. Those living appeared dead, their starving bodies struggling to walk hopelessly to their destinations.

Rose helped Cila navigate the bridge's steep steps, keeping up with traffic. They continued on Lutomierska Street, heading towards their apartment. Cila was shaking uncontrollably. Rose opened her coat, picked up Cila, and buttoned it around them. She thought about life before the ghetto. Fitting them into a coat together would have been impossible. Now, even though Cila had grown, there was more than enough room.

The unusual sight caught the eye of two German soldiers walking in the opposite direction on Lutomierska. Rose saw them eyeing her and picked up the pace. The Germans crossed the street and called out to her.

"Halt, Jew!" one of them yelled.

Not wanting to stop, Rose picked up her pace to a light jog.

"Jew, get back here," the other soldier called out.

Realizing Rose was not going to stop, the soldiers, now infuriated with the disobedience of ghetto-dwelling Jews, chased after them.

Rose carrying Cila was no match for two trained soldiers. In thirty seconds, the soldiers caught up and forcefully pushed them into a brick wall.

"I ordered you to stop!" screamed one of the soldiers.

"I thought you were talking to someone else," responded Rose, apologetically.

"Then why were you running?" the other soldier asked.

Thinking fast, Rose answered, "She's cold and heavy and I wanted to get her home quickly."

"Well then, allow me to help," the first soldier responded, smiling.

He reached down to Rose's raggedy coat and yanked it apart. The buttons vanished into the slushy street. Rose screamed for him to stop and for somebody to help. People looked away, fearful that watching or helping would drag them into it. Rose could not blame them: she had done the same in the past.

Cila clung on to her mother tightly as the soldier attempted to pull them apart. She screamed "Ema, Ema," as her nails dug into Rose's neck for dear life. When her fragile hands lost grip of Rose's neck, she latched onto the torn coat. Rose wailed for the soldiers to stop.

Cila's grip slipped from the coat. Rose reached out, grabbing onto Cila's hands. One soldier refused to give up pulling on Cila, whose eyes filled with fear and tears. The second soldier kicked Rose hard in the gut but she continued to hold on to her daughter. Rose lost her wind on the next kick, falling down to the street and letting go of Cila.

The German carried Cila across the street. She screamed "Ema, Ema," at the top of her lungs. Out of fear and desperation, Cila kicked the soldier and scratched his face. Rose found the energy to get up and chase them.

The soldier wound back and threw Cila over the barbed wire fence. Before she cleared the top, a rifle shot went off, dramatically changing the direction her body was heading. Rose shrieked as she saw her daughter hanging upside down, her dress caught on a few barbs. Blood dripped off her head onto the white untouched snow on the outer side of the ghetto fence.

Rose reached up to touch her daughter's lifeless hand. The warmth embracing it moments earlier already began to fade. The soldier who shot Cila kneed Rose in her side. She fell down to the street and stayed there, afraid to move.

"We've lightened your load, now here's some warmth," said the soldier, undoing his pant zipper and urinating on her.

Rose sat next to Cila on the side of the road for a few minutes. Seeing no Germans in the perimeter, people walked by looking at her with empathy. She said goodbye to her beautiful daughter and made her way to the Znamirowski apartment, waiting next to Esther until Touba and Simcha arrived.

Teddy backed away from the door, understanding what he heard. His heart sank. Teddy and Cila were close. He played with her and considered her another sister. He never imagined life without Cila. A twelve-year-old did not think that way.

He walked upstairs to Kwart's apartment and faked a smile, pretending he had no idea what had happened.

#

11: We're So Hungry

The news hit the family hard. Death was everywhere but no one in the immediate family had passed before Cila. Esther was overwhelmed, and cried uncontrollably. The fact Cila was the same age took away all feelings of immunity. She now thought about two things during her long days at home: food and Cila.

Chuh Chuh Rose was now disheveled and pacing the tiny apartment. Next to her sister-in-law, Cila was the only immediate family she had left and now she was gone.

At the start of the German invasion, Rose's husband, Touba's brother, had left town to establish himself elsewhere so Rose and Cila had a place to go if the Germans advanced to Lodz. Before he made it to his destination, the German army surrounded him.

Soldiers locked Rose's husband and his travelling companions in a barn, and set it ablaze. Trapped inside, they all burned to death except one man from their group who had been peeing in the woods. Seeing their demise, he felt obligated to return to Lodz and tell their families.

Rose was lost without Cila. She isolated herself from everything. She worked for her soup and then returned to her apartment. The ghetto had finally won its battle.

The cold grew unforgiving as it fell deeper into winter. Icicles hung from the ends of rooftops like teeth waiting to bite down on weary victims. Snow piled up on street corners, taking every opportunity to remind passing inhabitants of the season's cruelness.

The minimal coal ration was insufficient to fend off the cold. It was not enough to cook soup let alone heat an entire apartment, forcing everyone to make do with what was available, regardless of the conditions.

Frigid temperatures chilled Teddy and Simcha to the bone as they walked home holding their family's eight-day food supply.

"I remember when your mom and I couldn't carry the food for the two of us for eight days, and now look," said Simcha. "Now it's you and I, Tanchum, carrying food for five with room to spare."

"I'm so hungry, Abba," responded Teddy.

"I know you are, Tanchum. We all are," said Simcha, leaning over to give Teddy a reassuring hug.

When they arrived home, Touba was waiting to unpack the food. The canned beets were frozen.

"What the hell are we supposed to do with these?" said Simcha. "We're going to burn more energy opening the can than eating the contents."

Teddy reached into the bag and pulled out potatoes, which were also frozen. He gave Simcha a distressed look, showing him the frozen potatoes.

"Those are too?" Simcha exclaimed. "We have next to no food and what we do have, we cannot eat!"

Pola and Esther sat on the bed shivering, covered in blankets. Coal, everyone agreed, was strictly for cooking and barely lasted for that. Teddy and Simcha climbed under the blankets with the family. They brought the canned beets and potatoes with them, hoping their body heat might soften them.

Temperatures outside continued to decline daily. People found any means possible to create heat. Frostbite was widespread.

The Znamirowskis heard banging in the apartment hallway. Teddy forced himself to part with the small amount of warmth he'd gained with his family to check on it. Though unusual, the sight made sense.

Neighbors were taking their wooden front doors off to burn as a source of heat. Quickly, Simcha and Teddy joined everyone else, taking off their own door and replacing it with a blanket. Teddy decided he would scavenge the surrounding area for anything burnable to stay warm.

He walked along Wrobla Street, breaking off a few reachable tree branches and picking a few off the ground. *I need to find a better source of materials*, Teddy decided. Walking around, he saw people with the same idea.

They were pulling apart an old wooden rundown shack to burn in their fires. Teddy ran home with his branches and told Simcha what he'd seen. Together, they rushed to the shack. Most of the disassembling had already occurred by the time they arrived. They carried home as many pieces of wood as possible in their two trips before the shack vanished.

Teddy and Pola no longer slept on the floor. All five Znamirowskis crowded into the tiny bed, using their body warmth as heat. It was painful to get out of bed in the morning. Bitter cold air in the apartment met the comforting warmth generated by the family's bodies harshly. It took Teddy five minutes to get his body functional enough to accomplish his morning routine.

As Teddy pushed the frozen blanket that doubled as a front door aside, there were loud cracks as ice broke and fell and shattered on the floor. He took his family's urine and feces-filled bucket and dumped it by the fence on Gnieznienska Street when no one was looking. The family had started using the bucket after temperatures dropped so low inside the apartment that the toilet water froze.

After work one day, Kwart asked Teddy to carry a jar of gourmet jam to a judge living across town. He needed to stay home with Anna, who had developed pneumonia, but also desperately needed to deliver the jam. Feeling guilty he could no longer smuggle antibiotics to help her, Teddy agreed.

Trudging through dirty snow and slush, Teddy's hunger got the better of him. Without thinking, he pried open the lid to the strawberry jam and used his finger to scoop it into his mouth. The taste blew Teddy's mind. It had been two years since he'd tasted something so flavorful and sweet. Only in his dreams could he remember what jam tasted like. It was the best thing he'd ever experienced. Teddy felt sugar coursing through his veins. He walked to the judge's residence with an extra bounce in his stride.

Teddy took another taste, then another. He felt like a kid again, a permanent grin stuck on his face, as if he was eating sweets for the first time. By the time he reached the judge's apartment, half the jar was empty. He knew the consequences of his actions would be dire but it was too late to erase what happened. He could not replace the jam. It was not cheap or easy to come by. The punishment was likely to be severe – probably a beating or, worse, withholding his family's rations.

Teddy desperately looked around for a way out of his mess. He thought of not delivering the jam to the judge, but that would get Kwart into trouble since he should have delivered it. He contemplated making a story about a mugging, but it would be a hard story to prove, especially when everyone would think he ate it anyway.

He gazed at the apartment building, then to his left and right, but nothing came to mind. An icicle hanging from a window ledge guided his eyes down like a finger pointing to the ground. At his feet was snow, and plenty of it. *That's it!* Teddy thought. He scooped some snow into the jar, stirring with his finger to blend it in. He wiped the sides of the jar to give it a cleaner-looking appearance and put the lid back on tightly to make the delivery.

On the walk home, Teddy was in his glory. The unexpected rush of sugar had put him into a euphoric state. His mind took him out of the ghetto to his childhood, when eating jam was not a luxury. He thought of the field across from his apartment and the games he and his friends used to play. Life was carefree and simple.

When he got home, he did not tell anyone about the jam.

The next day, Simcha barreled through the blanketed front door. The ice released its tight grip on the blanket, shattering as it fell to the floor.

"Rumkowski is ordering another set of wedding invitations to be sent out," he declared.

Wedding invitations was the term used for notices for deportation.

Touba was sitting with the children at the table and quickly stood up on hearing the news.

"Who are they requesting to deport now?" asked Touba, concerned.

"I don't know yet," Simcha responded, "but they've already taken all the gypsies and criminals. I don't think they're too specific anymore."

"Where do the people go, Abba?" asked Esther.

"I don't know, *mine sheyn ponem*, but we're going to stay right here," said Simcha, making his best attempt to comfort her.

Touba and Simcha looked at each other, fear in their eyes. They did not know what the deportations meant or where they headed. They only knew they needed to keep the family together. Life in the ghetto was beyond terrible, but at least they understood what they were dealing with. The fear of the unknown was terrifying.

Rumors spread around the ghetto about deportations. Some were good and some not so good. Miriam, who worked next to Pola in the factory, spoke of deportations as relocation somewhere out east for forced labor. Jacov, who worked with Teddy and Chaim, mentioned that those deported received a meal during their travels.

"Who wouldn't want that?" Jacov said, enthusiastically.

Some men at the boot factory with Simcha spoke of horrible endings to those who left. Rumors of torture, endless hard labor and immediate death circulated around the factory.

"They're taking a thousand people a day," said Simcha. "It would be impossible to kill them all."

Simcha stayed positive and hoped things would get better. Since Lodz' occupation, he had constantly prayed for the situation to improve or, at the very least, not get worse. His prayers went unanswered and his family's situation deteriorated. The thought of meeting death soon after leaving Lodz was the ultimate destination on the steady decline their life had taken. Simcha tried to keep the faith – to believe this was not the end. Life was at its lowest point and he could not see it getting any worse.

"They wouldn't waste that many bullets on us," said Avram, working across from Simcha. "They need us to provide uniforms and supplies. We are important," he continued.

Avram and Simcha were like-minded, always keeping a positive attitude. He too found it hard to believe the Germans would be too quick to dispose of them.

To Avram's right, Izaak chimed in. "Then why do they kill us at will and starve us to death. *Feh* with your positive thinking, *feh*."

When Simcha and Touba got home, the children were waiting for them. Esther devoured her half of Touba's soup without taking time to breathe. Lack of food took its toll on everyone, but her little body suffered the most. When everyone went to work, they interacted with other people and tried to keep their minds off food. Esther sat home all day obsessing about the lack of it. It was a chore for her to get up and move around the apartment. She was an eight year old trapped inside an eighty-year-old body.

Simcha sat down at the table staring blankly at his family. His body was in the apartment but his mind was elsewhere.

How can we avoid deportation? he asked himself.

"Tanchum, come with me," he said, standing up and heading towards the blanket-covered front door.

They headed down to the basement of the apartment building. It was a dank, cold room with a dirt floor, stone walls and a few tiny windows allowing a little light to enter. The children were terrified of the basement. Living on the first floor, they heard strange sounds arising from the basement. Pola was convinced it was haunted. The smells and dim light added to the scary atmosphere.

Simcha looked around, seeing if anything was usable. The basement was empty except for a pile of dry leaves and a few sheets of tin in one corner.

"What are we doing down here, Abba?" asked Teddy.

"One moment, *mine yingl*," Simcha responded.

He knelt down on the floor, gently scratching at its surface. The packed dirt came loose with a little effort. Simcha stood up and headed towards the stairs.

"Stay here, Tanchum. I'll be right back."

Simcha ran up the stairs, leaving Teddy by himself. Not wanting any part of being in the basement alone, Teddy ran to the top of the steps and sat there. Looking down into the darkness, he heard strange noises. The pile of leaves started rustling as strange shadows danced on the walls.

Teddy tried to convince himself his imagination was getting the better of him, but it did not help. The rustling of leaves grew louder, matching the beating of Teddy's heart.

A monster jumped out and ran towards him. Teddy gathered enough energy to get off the stairs and hide behind the door before almost fainting. His knees buckled underneath him as he forced himself to keep his eyes open.

The mouse ran up the stairs, down the hallway and out the front door. Teddy sighed and chuckled to himself at how he'd reacted to the situation. He returned to the stairs and waited for his father.

Simcha arrived a moment later with the bucket they used for a toilet, two serving spoons and two forks. He handed one spoon and fork to Teddy and told him to go downstairs.

"What are we doing with these?" asked Teddy, looking at the eating utensils, confused.

"We're going to dig," Simcha answered. "Come, watch me."

Simcha knelt on the floor and used his fork as a mini pickaxe to chop at the dirt. Teddy knelt beside him, following his lead. When enough dirt was loose, Teddy and Simcha used the serving spoons to shovel it into the bucket.

To avoid drawing attention to their task, they never brought the bucket holding dirt outside. Instead, Teddy spread the dirt over the floor and stepped on it to compact it into the ground.

After two months of digging, Simcha and Teddy had completed their task. They had dug a hole in the basement floor two feet deep, seven feet long and six feet wide, matching the length and width of the tin sheets stacked up on the wall.

"Hopefully we never have to use this," said Simcha.

Teddy and Chaim walked to the toy factory the next day. They'd survived the brutal winter in the most abysmal conditions imaginable, but the warm weather only melted the snow and did nothing to better their situation.

Chaim was having trouble walking, constantly bending over and grabbing his stomach.

"What's the matter?" asked Teddy.

"Nothing," answered Chaim, denying the pain that was eating his stomach.

The boys continued towards the factory and were a block away when Chaim began sobbing.

"What's the matter, Chaim?" said Teddy, a little more sternly this time.

Chaim leaned on the brick wall to his right, trying to avoid peeling plaster falling down on him.

"It's my father," said Chaim. "He's stealing all of my family's food."

"How could he do that?" asked Teddy.

"That greedy bastard said it's because he's the man of the family and needs more," answered Chaim. "Piece of *drek*, I can't even look at him."

He pushed himself off the wall and continued walking to the factory. Every step was agony as his body craved food for energy.

Teddy shared his almost all-liquid soup with Chaim, attempting to stave off his hunger and take the edge off the pain. Watching him drink made Teddy's stomach churn and the desire to take the bowl back grew strong, but he knew Chaim needed it. He could not get through this without his friend.

On the walk home, everyone heard a single gunshot. Not a soul in the starving mass of people flinched at the sound. They all knew a life had ended but they were numb. There was good and bad in the ghetto, but something more dreadful had taken over the weary souls who spent their existence there: indifference.

#

12: Remember Your Name

"Simcha, we need to go, now!" yelled Kwart through the blanket door to their apartment.

"What is it?" asked Simcha.

"Something is happening at the hospital," returned Kwart. "I need you to come with me."

Kwart, Simcha and Teddy ran to the hospital at 75 Drewnowska Street. As they got closer, the roar of the crowd escalated. A mob had gathered by the entrance, everyone struggling to get in the building. Teddy had not seen so much energy from ghetto inhabitants since before winter and the reason soon became clear.

Open-air cabin trucks lined the road like hungry beasts waiting for their next meal. Some of the hospital's occupants already sat in a few of them. Germans forcefully pushed others out of the front door towards the vehicles. Many of them were bleeding and Teddy assumed this was from strikes with rifle butts for not co-operating.

Kwart and Simcha pushed their way through the crowd. Kwart's mother-in-law Sala was in the hospital, having contracted typhus a week earlier. They got to the front of the mob and headed for the hospital door, but the soldiers working crowd control pushed them back into the throng of people.

Teddy arrived next to Simcha, unable to believe what he was seeing. He felt like he was watching an evil circus. One German grabbed an old man from his wheelchair and threw him to the ground. Laughing as the dreadfully weak man attempted to lift himself back into his chair, the German kicked him down again and stomped on him. Another patient who had been dragged out the door, pushed his captor and ran, hoping to blend in to the crowd. The soldier raised his gun and shot him before he had made it more than three steps.

A few people, having no fight left, walked gracefully to the trucks, accepting their fate.

"Do you see Sala, Simcha?" asked Kwart.

"No, not yet," replied Simcha. "She'll be ok," he continued, reassuring Kwart.

It did not work. The look on Kwart's face was one that no amount of reassuring could remove.

"My God, I put my son in the hospital because I thought he'd be safer," said a sobbing woman next to Teddy.

"My daughter is in there, too," another woman cried.

Teddy scanned the open area guarded by the German soldiers. A few of the dead bodies looked out of place. They appeared as healthy as one could hope to be after living two years in the ghetto's harsh conditions. Those victims had tried blending in with the sick in hopes of avoiding deportation, unaware that the hospital was the first area selected for liquidation.

Screams erupted in the crowd as they witnessed patients jumping out of windows to the street below. Germans threw those who did not leap voluntarily. The sound of bodies hitting the sidewalk left an uneasy feeling in Teddy. Trying to keep down what little food was in his stomach, he turned away.

Shots rang out from inside the building. After most of the patients had been loaded into the trucks, soldiers patrolled the hospital wings, searching for any in hiding, trying to avoid deportation.

The vehicles drove off as the parents of children onboard trailed behind, screaming the names of their loved ones. Soldiers shot a few down. Others gave up and stood hopelessly in the street, knowing it was a lost cause.

It was a long walk back to Gnieznienska Street for Kwart, who feared he had lost his mother-in-law.

"You didn't see her, right?" he asked repeatedly.

"No, maybe she got away," answered Simcha, staying positive.

When Kwart entered his apartment, Anna saw he was without her mother and began sobbing.

"I didn't get to say goodbye," she cried.

Kwart spared Anna the details of what he had witnessed in front of the hospital.

"I didn't see her board any trucks, my love," said Kwart, sitting next to his wife and putting his arm around her shoulders.

Anna's sister, Rebekah, sat next to them silently. She stared out the window with a blank look on her face, struggling with her own fears.

Leaving the family to mourn, Simcha and Teddy returned to their apartment to tell their family what they had seen.

"Things are far worse than we could have expected," said Simcha.

"They even threw people out of windows," Teddy added, shuddering at the memory.

Pola grabbed her mother's elbow with one hand and reached down with the other to hold Esther, who nervously played with Anka's hair.

"So they took Sala then?" asked Touba.

"We don't know for sure, but we assume so, yes," answered Simcha.

"God protect her," responded Touba.

A few days later, Kwart knocked on the wall next to the hanging blanket of the Znamirowski apartment.

"Come in," called Simcha.

Kwart walked in, taking off his raggedy hat. He looked as if he had seen a ghost. He shuffled to the table, pulling out a chair to sit down. His hands shook as he placed his hat down.

"What's the matter?" asked Simcha, concerned with Kwart's behavior.

Kwart looked up. Finding it hard to maintain eye contact, he shifted his focus to the floor. He nervously rocked in the chair, contemplating how to answer Simcha's question.

"Rumkowski made a speech," said Kwart.

"Yeah, he always does," responded Simcha, sarcastically.

"This one was different," replied Kwart. "He asked parents to give up their children for deportation."

"You're kidding me," answered Simcha, incredulous.

"I wish I was," said Kwart. "He's requesting children under ten, the elderly over sixty-five and anyone unable to work for deportation."

Simcha immediately thought of his precious little Esther.

"This can't be happening," said Simcha.

Posters hung around the ghetto announcing the *Allgemeine Gehsperre*, which placed everyone under house arrest. Anyone caught outside faced deportation or worse.

Kwart, being part of the Jewish police and security for a judge, had participated in round-ups and selection of Jews for deportation. The thought of selecting children turned his stomach.

"I'll give you a heads-up when they are coming to our area," Kwart told the Znamirowskis.

Everyone dealt with his or her fear of deportation differently. Some families accepted their fate with hopes it may be a little better than their current situation, although they doubted it. Nothing got better anymore.

Other families went into hiding, crawling into or behind any structure or crevice that would shield them. Boxes, attic crawl spaces, floorboards, closets and other areas became sanctuaries – places where people prayed they would be safe. Places where people prayed for their lives.

The Ginsberg family on the fourth floor of the Znamirowski apartment building had three children, all under the age of ten. Rather than have Germans come destroy their family, Saul and Rachel decided on a collective family suicide.

Saul went to each of his children. He kissed them on both cheeks and atop their foreheads. He told them he would see them soon and that he loved them.

He went to Rachel, giving her a long hug and kiss.

"I love you, Rachele," said Saul. "We've had a good life together, I'll see you soon."

Saul watched each of his family members eat their final pieces of bread laced with poison. After they passed away, he lifted them carefully and laid them gently in their bed.

He covered them with blankets and kissed them each one more time. Saul took a step back and looked at his family. They seemed so peaceful. He proceeded to climb to the roof of the apartment building. He slowly walked to the edge, looking at the sky one last time before closing his eyes and stepping off the side.

The Znamirowskis had a plan of their own. They would wait for Kwart to tell them the Germans were on their way and then run down to the basement and hide in the hole Simcha and Teddy had dug a few months earlier until inspection and round-ups were complete.

That night, screams came from the second floor. Simcha sat up in a panic, thinking Germans were in the building, but he quickly relaxed, remembering that they rarely rounded people up at night.

"Simcha," a voice called out from the hallway. "Simcha, come quickly."

This time he got out of bed and walked to the blanket-covered doorway. His heart raced with anticipation for the reason of his summons.

"Are they coming?" asked Simcha, recognizing Kwart's voice.

"No, but you need to see this," answered Kwart.

They walked upstairs into Kwart's apartment. Simcha rubbed his eyes in disbelief.

"Sala?" said Simcha, as if he had seen a ghost.

He ran to Kwart's mother-in-law, and hugged her.

"How is this possible?" asked Simcha, still amazed to see her in front of him.

Sala had heard the trucks pull up to the hospital. She'd got out of bed and walked to the window to see what was happening. Seeing the Germans run into the building, she assumed the worst and frantically searched for a hiding spot.

She ended up finding an unlocked supply closet storing mops, cleaning supplies and soiled bed linens. Quickly, Sala moved the sheets to hide under. In doing so, she uncovered a small closet door against the wall at the far end of the pile. She opened the door and crept inside, placing the sheets back in front before closing herself in.

On two occasions, Germans opened the closet to search for stragglers. Sala heard bayonets piercing through the sheets covering the hidden door, but the soldiers never noticed the door itself. She waited in the closet for hours before the hospital fell silent. She then crawled out, wrapping herself in a sheet and putting a pillowcase over the top of her shaved head to conceal the fact she was coming from the hospital.

During the dead of night, fearful of being outdoors after curfew, Sala had gradually gone from apartment to apartment for shelter, slowly making her way back to Gnieznienska Street.

She arrived the next morning, to everyone's disbelief and excitement.

"We thought the worst," said Touba, giving her a hug.

"It'll take more than that for Kwart to get rid of me," Sala joked.

The reunion was short-lived. The neighing of horses accompanied by wooden wheels on cobblestone made everyone jump to attention. A few seconds later, the angry barks of dogs and Germans alike told everyone to move quickly.

The entire apartment building came to life, like thousands of bees leaving the hive after being disturbed. Floors creaked as people scurried around to get ready for inspection or find a place to hide. Kwart glanced at Simcha with an apologetic expression. He had known nothing about the raid and had figured that being at the edge of the smaller ghetto area put them at the end of the list. He'd had no way to warn them.

With no time to get to their basement hiding spot, the Znamirowskis ran to their apartment. They threw on as many layers of clothes as they could to look heavier and healthier than they were. Touba went around pinching her children's cheeks to bring some color to their pale, starving faces.

Esther shook, fighting back her tears, while holding firmly onto Anka. A few escaped and Touba used them to her advantage, wiping Esther's face clean. She combed everyone's hair, leaving no time to get herself ready.

The Germans barged through the blanketed doorway to find the Znamirowskis standing shoulder to shoulder. The Doberman Pincer led the way, walking straight to Esther. He smelled her for a few seconds and spent extra time on Anka. He licked Esther's hand, causing his owner to yank forcefully on the leash. The dog yelped and returned to his master's side.

One soldier walked around inspecting the family. He took his time, knowing he controlled their destiny. Screaming upstairs confirmed that the Germans were already making decisions and tearing families apart, destroying their lives.

Dawid raced down from the third floor, chasing after a soldier who was carrying his son away.

"Give me back my boy!" he screamed.

His argument ended quickly with a bullet dropping his lifeless body down the stairs. It landed in front of the Znamirowski apartment.

The soldier holding on to the Doberman inspected the room, making sure nobody was hiding. When he was done, he nodded to another soldier who began his selection.

He grabbed Esther by the hand and pulled her forward. The situation finally became too much for her and she began sobbing hysterically.

"*Oy vey*," left Touba's mouth as she watched the German select her daughter for deportation.

"No!" screamed Pola, extending her arms to her sister.

A desperate Esther screamed for her mother.

The soldier paid no attention to the family, having heard the same pleas from others. He walked up to Teddy, grabbed his arm and yanked him forward in a similar fashion to Esther.

Realizing he had been selected, Teddy called out, "But I am over ten".

The German disregarded him. The age requirement was a guideline. Years of malnourishment and extreme hardships had changed Teddy's body to that of an eight or nine year old. He was strong but skinny and appeared young and unhealthy to the soldier, which meant deportation.

Simcha wept. It was the first time in years his children had seen him cry, but thoughts of losing any of them, let alone two, was more than he could handle. He began pleading with the Germans to let his family stay. They ignored him.

The soldier did one more walk around of the Znamirowski family. He reached out grabbing Touba's arm and tugged her forward too.

When the wagons pulled up in front of the apartment, Touba had spent all her time making sure the family was prepared and looking healthy but had done nothing to take care of herself. Years in the ghetto had taken a heavy toll on her. She had lost a lot of weight, and, although she was only forty-two, she appeared much older.

Touba was not surprised at her selection. She feared the worst, but knew wherever she went she would be able to look after her two youngest while Simcha watched over Pola.

The Germans proceeded to push Touba, Teddy and Esther towards the blanketed doorway and outside to the horse-drawn wagon. When they reached the front door of the apartment building, Pola could no longer contain herself. She ran towards her family, screaming at the soldiers to allow them to stay or take her with them.

The soldiers paid no attention to her as they loaded Esther, clinging to Anka, onto the wagon. Once aboard, she sat next to a child separated from his family. When Teddy and Touba boarded the wagon, Pola reached forward and tugged hard on a soldier's sleeve. Screaming did not get his attention, but pulling on his uniform certainly did. The thought of a dirty Jew touching his impeccable outfit angered him. He turned around, grabbed Pola by her hair and dragged her to the last truck in line, throwing her onboard.

Simcha could not comprehend what he witnessed. In a matter of seconds, he had lost his wife and two youngest children to the deportation. Now they had taken his oldest daughter as well. A feeling of emptiness overwhelmed him as he heard horse hooves on cobblestone streets and watched large wagons take his entire family away.

Teddy, Touba and Esther got off at the hospital on Drewnowska Street. The mere sight of the place sent violent chills down Teddy's spine. He thought about the disappearance of Hana Minski. Even fresher in his mind was the liquidation of the hospital a few days earlier and the sight of people falling from its windows.

Pola, certain she would be reunited with her family, went to a separate holding station at the central prison. Realizing her efforts had not worked in her favor, she put her head in her hands and sobbed, not knowing if she would ever see her family again.

The horse-drawn wagons continued bringing children, the elderly and those unable to work to the hospital. People were confined by fences, and could not leave the holding area. For the first time in years, fear and nervousness overtook thoughts of hunger.

After three long days of waiting without food or toilets, the deportations began. The roaring of trucks outside signaled the Jews that their time had come.

"Where are we going, Ema?" asked Esther, her voice laced with fear.

"I don't know, my child," answered Touba.

"I hope it's someplace better then here," said Esther.

"Me too, Etelle. Me too," said Touba, grabbing Esther close. She took a deep breath in and exhaled slowly.

A child, no more than eight, left the line, running towards a fence and began to climb. A German grabbed him and threw him back to the line. Another German shot a child before she reached the fence.

As they moved closer to the trucks, the smell of diesel filled their noses, making them dizzy. Surrounded by children and the elderly, Touba was the tallest person around, giving her a clear view.

The Germans loaded children first, laying them on the floor. Next, the elderly and unfit to work boarded, forced to stand on top of the small, fragile bodies. Children screamed for the adults to get off but there was no room to move. The cries eventually died down as they realized they needed to conserve their energy to breathe with the heavy weight on them.

Once a truck was loaded, the doors slammed shut and they headed north to Radegast Station in the Marysin section. From there, the Jews would board trains and exit the ghetto.

As she watched the Germans load people on the trucks, Touba's instincts kicked in. Her eyes gazed upon the dead body lying by the fence. She hesitated, thinking about consequences should her son be caught, but knew it was worth the risk. She believed in her boy. Touba tried hard to swallow past the lump in her throat then turned to face Teddy.

"Tanchum, you must listen to me," said Touba, scoping her surroundings for Germans. The line picked up pace.

"Yes, Ema," answered Teddy obediently.

Children inside trucks shrieked in the background as adults stood on top of them. Urgency filled Touba's voice.

"Can you make it to the apartment?"

Teddy stared at his mother, confused. He turned to view the line behind him then scanned the surrounding area for an escape route. He noted the locations of the Germans, then faced his mother again.

"I can make it," Teddy answered.

"Good," said Touba.

She reached out with her loving arm and placed it on his shoulder. Holding back tears to be strong for her son, her voice cracked as she spoke.

"You must run, Tanchum. Get out of here. Get back to the apartment," said Touba quickly as time ran out. "Remember what you see here and who you are. You are special, Tanchum, a survivor. Tell your father everything. Remember your family. Now run. Run, and remember your name."

With no time to hesitate, Teddy leaned over and kissed Esther. He knelt down and gave Anka a kiss, making his sister smile. He turned to face Touba. Without saying a word, he leaned in and hugged his mom, closing his eyes and inhaling her scent deeply to grasp one more thing to remember her by. He then kissed both of her cheeks.

Teddy stepped back taking in one more glance of his mother and younger sister. He looked up at Touba and nodded, confirming a mutual understanding.

Using the long line of children and adults behind him, Teddy walked backwards through the crowd. Every time a soldier looked at the line, he stopped and slowly moved ahead with the group. He used his method of blending in until turning the corner of the hospital where no soldiers were present.

Teddy turned and bolted towards the fence, which he scaled with ease. He ran into a building across the street and shut the door behind him. The realization that he had likely said goodbye to his mother and sister forever took hold, and he began crying uncontrollably.

He dropped to the floor, leaning his head on his knees. Thoughts of future memories that would never happen flooded Teddy's mind. His mother's cooking, her smell, her voice, sitting down at the dinner table together, Esther combing Anka's hair, playing hide and seek, teaching her jump rope. The teasing his sisters put him through, which had irked him endlessly, was now all he desired.

Not wanting to let his mother down, Teddy regained his composure and made his way back to Simcha. He stuck to the insides of buildings to avoid detection. The *Gehsperre* was still in effect and no one allowed outside.

Teddy was approaching the wooden bridge on Lutomierska Street when a strong hand grabbed him, yanking him violently into an alleyway. Fearing the worst, Teddy turned around and almost fainted with relief upon seeing who it was.

Kwart was patrolling the streets to make sure Jews obeyed the *Gehsperre*. By chance, he happened to be in the right place, spotting Teddy before he crossed over the bridge.

"Look what we have here," said Kwart, wiping a tear from his eye. "I thought I'd never see you again."

Teddy explained the hospital scene to Kwart and that he needed to get back to his father.

"I'll get you across," said Kwart. "You're lucky we bumped into each other. The Germans would have certainly shot you as you crossed the bridge. No one is allowed outside."

Kwart told Teddy to ready himself for a beating while crossing over to make the scenario appear more realistic to the guards.

They neared the bridge when a German soldier standing at its entrance eyed them curiously. Kwart punched Teddy in his shoulder then kicked him in the back of his knee, dropping him to the street.

"Stupid Jew," he yelled, picked him back up and pushed him forward. "I'm taking him to the central prison," Kwart told the guard as they crossed over the bridge.

They made it safely to Gnieznienska Street. Teddy ran though the blanket door yelling "Abba" at the top of his lungs. Simcha, depressed and beside himself at having lost his entire family, lay in the bed they had all shared. He jumped up upon hearing his son's voice. Running into the kitchen, he lifted Teddy into his arms.

"*Mine yingl, mine yingl*," Simcha said repeatedly, staring at his precious child. "How did you come back to me?"

Teddy explained the situation to Simcha, whose eyes welled up, wondering about the future of his family.

"Come, we must conceal you," said Simcha.

They headed to the hole in the basement where they had originally planned to hide. Teddy climbed in and laid flat. Simcha walked to the corner of the room and grabbed aluminum sheets and leaves. He placed a sheet over the hole, covered it with a layer of the dried brush, and repeated the process until all the available resources were gone.

The place Teddy once feared the most was now the safest. Nothing down there scared him more than the Germans outside. The basement now became a place of comfort he did not want to leave.

Two days later, three soldiers entered the building to search for stragglers. After finding the apartments empty, two of the soldiers headed down to the basement. Except for the small pile of leaves near the center, the room was vacant. One soldier fixed a bayonet to his rifle while approaching the leaves and struck downward into the pile twice.

The first strike missed Teddy but the second blow nicked his forearm. He bit down hard on his lower lip to stop himself from making a sound. A tear fell from his eye, but he remained quiet and the German did not notice.

As the soldiers walked upstairs, Simcha peered out of his apartment's blanketed doorway. At first, the bayonet scared him as he had not heard a gunshot, but seeing no blood on the blade and noticing the soldiers' demeanor led him to believe Teddy was safe.

"Do you know something?" one of the soldiers asked Simcha.

Teddy held one hand to his wound, lifting himself up with the other to listen in on the conversation.

"I know nothing," responded Simcha, looking down to avoid eye contact at all costs.

One soldier grabbed Simcha by his shirt and pulled him out of his apartment.

"Do you think he knows something?" the German asked his comrade.

"Yes I think he knows something," the other soldier responded.

"I know nothing, please let me go," pleaded Simcha.

"I'm afraid I cannot do that," said the soldier, tightening his grip on Simcha's shirt. "You are coming with us."

Teddy pressed up firmly on the aluminum muffling the conversation.

"Everything has its price," said Simcha.

Then silence.

#

13: Thirteen-Year-Old Man

"You mean Saba lost his whole family?" asked Hayden, looking at me through the rearview mirror.

"Yes, he did, Hayden. They were all taken from him," I responded.

"I don't think I could live without you guys," said Hayden, shifting her gaze to her mother.

"We couldn't live without you either," responded Shannon.

"How did he survive?" Hayden asked, interested in learning more.

I smiled, happy she was interested in her great-grandfather's story.

Teddy lay in his hole covered by aluminum and leaves. A few hours passed and he began wondering why his father had not retrieved him. *Where is he? Did they really take him away? Will he come back? Is he —?* He strained his ears to hear his father's voice, but heard nothing. *Something terrible must have happened if he hasn't come back by now*, Teddy thought.

Listening carefully to his surroundings, nobody spoke German and he did not hear dogs barking. There was only silence. He quietly shifted the aluminum and climbed out of his hiding place. He covered it up, unsure if he would need to use it again soon.

As Teddy walked up the basement stairs, a strange feeling overtook him. He was now completely dependent on himself. In the seconds it had taken the soldiers to whisk Simcha away, Teddy, still only thirteen, became an adult.

He peeked out of the front door, checking to see if anyone was nearby. The streets were empty and eerily quiet. Voices inside the building whispered, "They got Znamirowski." Teddy turned and headed for his apartment.

Simcha's bread lay on the kitchen table. Teddy had not eaten in days and part of him wanted to leave it, hoping his father would return, but deep inside he knew he was gone. He wolfed the bread down quickly, sitting at the table and thinking about his life before heading to bed.

A few years ago, Teddy had bragged to his sisters about how he was lucky to have his own bedroom when they had to share one. The Germans had taken all that away, forcing his family to live in the tiny ghetto apartment where they shared one bed.

Teddy lay by himself, feeling alone. The full-sized bed that once held all five members of his family felt enormous with only his tiny body lying in it. He covered himself with a blanket, shivering from the lack of body warmth his family had supplied. *Will I ever see them again? What do I do now?* Unable to take it anymore, he rolled on his side and cried himself to sleep.

The *Gehsperre* was still in effect the next day. Teddy dragged his feet around the apartment lacking enthusiasm. The joy once pouring out of him had ceased to exist. His charisma that used to attract good things now brought only German hatred.

Teddy walked down the hallway of his building and headed upstairs. He walked past Kwart's room on the second floor, not bothering to stop by. He continued up the next flight of stairs to the third floor.

He passed doorways covered by blankets, as they had been ever since the bitter cold of the past winter. Inside an apartment, Teddy heard Rivka crying over the loss of her husband and son. Teddy had seen Dawid killed while trying to stop his son's deportation.

He made his way to the fourth floor and walked the long hallway. A thick dirt film nobody wanted to touch covered windows to the left. Perhaps it was too disgusting or maybe no one wanted to shed any light on the revolting conditions within.

To the right was the Ginsberg apartment where the wife and three children had left the confines of the ghetto. He understood their choice. They were all together. As Teddy walked past the apartment, a sense of calm came over him knowing that they no longer suffered.

He made his way to the roof. The sky was a beautiful blue. Teddy peered far into the distance over barbed wire fences to where people lived with a sense of normalcy. He saw posts where Germans kept watch on Jews during all hours of the day, shooting at them for sport or simply because they were bored.

Teddy neared the edge of the roof and looked down to the cobblestone street four stories below. He imagined the thoughts going through Saul's head before he leapt.

Teddy had lost his parents and both sisters in a matter of days. He did not know whether they were dead or alive, though he feared the worst. He longed to be with them. To see Esther holding Anka or watch Pola put on makeup. He yearned to smell Touba's cooking and help Simcha paint beautiful signs.

He lifted his leg to step off the roof when a voice shouted, "Don't."

Teddy, surprised someone was behind him, turned to see Kwart standing there.

"There's a reason you're here, Tanchum." said Kwart. "You're too young. Your father was taken so you could live."

Teddy, half-relieved Kwart had showed up to stop him, ran over and hugged him.

"I don't know what to do," said Teddy.

"I'm going to take care of you," answered Kwart.

Over the next few weeks, the ghetto turned into a full-force work camp. With the children, sick and elderly out of the area, everyone remaining worked under harsh conditions. Rations were stretched to last ten days instead of eight causing the numbers of dead to increase as starvation took its toll. Vegetables were non-existent.

Teddy adapted to his new life. Kwart and Anna took him in as family and tried their best to fill the void left in Teddy's heart by the deportation of his family. He no longer worked at the toy factory with Chaim, who had also made it through selections. The Germans handed lists of everyone taken during the *Gehsperre* to factory supervisors. Teddy's name was on the list. If he went to the factory, they would kill him. Chaim's father had been deported. Even though he was mad at his father for stealing food, Chaim still wanted him around.

Kwart found Teddy a job at the courthouse delivering mail and food to judges. Judges ate better than most and, like he had with the jam, Teddy continued sneaking pieces of food for himself. A small taste of marmalade or an extra bite of bread went a long way in boosting his morale.

Daily, he walked well out his way during his journey home from the courthouse to pass by the hospital. He did so, not to remind himself of the horrors that happened there, but to relive the last time he saw his mother and sister.

On a dreary day that could not decide when it was going to rain, Teddy walked by the hospital. It had been converted to the Knitted Goods Department and laundry center. Next to a side door was a pile of laundry ten feet tall.

The mountain of clothes drew Teddy near. Approaching the massive pile, he noticed a tiny hand sticking out next to a pair of pants. He reached down to tug at the hand and what appeared brought him to tears.

Anka had seen better days. The months she had been outside and uncared for had taken its toll on her already ragged body. Touba's stitches still held true, keeping her stuffing intact. Her hair was a knotted mess. Esther had combed it last.

Teddy scanned the area getting the feeling someone was watching him. Nobody was around. *How did this doll get here*? Teddy thought. He wondered if his mom and younger sister or his older sister and father were in the ghetto somewhere, unable to get back to Gnieznienska Street.

He sighed, lowering his head and knowing it was not the truth. He became saddened thinking how Esther did not have Anka with her, wherever she was. When Teddy got back to the apartment, he combed Anka's hair and placed her on a chair at the kitchen table, hoping that if he saw Esther again she'd be happy Anka had been well taken care of.

Hunger was all around. People walking to work collapsed dead on the street daily. Conditions inside factories grew worse as demands for production increased.

Chaim came home from the toy factory one day and told Teddy he'd witnessed something horrible. He described the terrible atmosphere at the factory now and told Teddy he was better off not working there.

Four soldiers and two men dressed in suits had been walking around the toy factory, inspecting the efficiency of its workers. The thick tension of the men's presence had everyone on edge. Chaim eyed them carefully. He doubled his work speed when they approached, showing them he could handle his job.

After twelve hours of hard labor, Chaim got ready to leave the factory now nicknamed the Toy Resort. All factories were resorts because they held opportunities to earn soup and get warm in winter, despite brutal working conditions.

He was heading for the exit when a single gunshot echoed through the factory. Everyone froze in his or her tracks, not knowing what was happening. In the doorway a boy lay face down, blood pooling in front of him.

Not knowing what to do, everyone stayed put, afraid to move. The boy's murderer walked over and lifted his body off the ground. He reached into his buttoned jacket, removed a wood spinning top, and showed it to the workers.

"Stealing will not be tolerated," said the soldier, before throwing the boy's body to the side. "These toys are not made for Jews."

Everyone rushed out of the factory avoiding the blood in the doorway.

The boy's name was Eljasz. He was twelve years old. His parents had successfully hidden his younger brother during the *Gehsperre* and had remained unselected themselves. Eljasz was only bringing the top home to show his parents what he did in the factory and to give his six-year-old brother something to play with because his parents did not permit him to leave the apartment, fearing deportation or worse.

The next day as workers walked into the factory, they saw Eljasz's body in a chair by the front door. String wrapped around his neck and torso and fastened to the wall by hooks held his body upright. The Germans had made the supervisor stay after everyone else had left to set up Eljasz's body. The young boy became a warning to deter anyone from stealing toys from the factory. Three days later, a soldier permitted workers to take his body down.

Back on Gnieznienska Street, Sala was losing her battle with the ghetto. The decrease in rations was taking a harsh toll on her already starving body and typhus played its part as well. She did not want to go back to the hospital, and rightly so, fearing another liquidation. She managed to get up every day and walk to work, certain that missing her soup would be the end of her.

The steep wooden steps of the bridge crossing Zgierska Street used to be no problem for her to climb. Now the staircase appeared as a mountain, impossible to conquer. Each step made her joints ache and muscles scream but the alternative was no soup and that was not going to happen. Day in and out, Sala walked to and from the factory, a shell of her former self, grasping on to whatever life she could.

In order to help with their food situation, Teddy took matters into his own hands. He became a creature of the night, leaving the apartment after dark to scrounge for anything edible. Knowing punishment was immediate death if caught outside after curfew, Teddy took extra precautions when he travelled, double-checking corners and streets before crossing.

Most nights he came home empty-handed but occasionally he returned with a potato or radish. One evening, Teddy set a trap for a horse-drawn cart carrying potatoes. As the cart drew near, Teddy jammed a thick stick in between the spokes of its wooden wheel, causing some of them to snap. The cart tipped in Teddy's direction dropping hundreds of potatoes through the barbed wire fence onto the ghetto's cobblestone street.

Hearing the crash, more than fifty people ran outside, braving the punishment of disobeying curfew, to grab as many potatoes as they could carry. It became a perfect cover for Teddy to escape undetected with twenty-six potatoes rolled in his shirt.

As summer approached, the heat made conditions worse. The ghetto was at its lowest point. Everyone was on the brink of death from starvation. The heat compounded the smells of urine and feces in the streets. Sweat stuck to the clothes of people who could not afford to wash them. The dead were everywhere.

"Hey Tanchum, do you remember Elzbieta Zielinski?" Chaim asked, walking around the ghetto one Sunday morning.

"Yeah, I remember her," said Teddy. "Why do you ask?"

"I had the biggest crush on her," answered Chaim. "She had the most beautiful brown hair."

"Yeah, she was pretty," agreed Teddy.

"What about the kiosk up the road from our old apartment, do you remember that?" asked Chaim.

Chaim reminisced to bring joy to the misery his life had become.

"Of course I do!" said Teddy with a little excitement in his voice. "I often think about what Tarzan is doing these days."

"Do you ever think things will go back to the way they were?" asked Chaim.

Teddy went to put his arm around Chaim and tell him he knew they would, but his arm fell on open air. Chaim was not there. The random bullet shot by a bored soldier struck Chaim as he finished asking his question, dropping him dead to the floor before Teddy could react.

Teddy did not dare turn around or stop walking to check on his best friend, fearing he would be next.

#

14: Where Are We Going?

At that moment, Teddy's life before the ghetto officially ended. Everyone he knew before the occupation was either dead or someplace he dared not go.

Chaim was his best friend. They had grown up together. They had gone on adventures and got into trouble together. Now, Chaim was dead. There was no reason for it. They had not been near a fence or trying to escape. They were two boys walking down the miserable streets of the ghetto. The guard patrolling the perimeter most likely wanted to see if his rifle worked and, with no regard for human life, had aimed at Chaim. Chaim had been taken from Teddy in an instant without a goodbye.

There was no time to mourn. Teddy ran back to Gneiznienka Street as quickly as he could. He headed upstairs to Kwart's apartment and sat there silently for an hour.

Teddy's mind played tricks on him the entire afternoon. He thought about the soldier pointing the rifle at him instead. Chaim was the lucky one. He did not have to deal with the ghetto any longer. Teddy wondered if Chaim was still in the street, or if a soldier had strung him up like Eljasz and used him as an example.

He snapped himself out of it. Thoughts like that poisoned people. Teddy paced up and down Gnieznienska Street, clearing his mind.

The next day Kwart announced to his Anna, Rebekah, Sala and Teddy, who had now been a member of Kwart's family for nearly two years, that another round of deportations was about to take place.

"What do you mean, another round?" asked Anna, worried.

"Who else can they deport?" questioned Rebekah.

Everyone turned to Sala, who looked out the window, but no one said a word. Sala's condition worsened daily but she would not admit it, using age as an excuse for her ailments.

"They're taking anyone," said Kwart. "But first, they want volunteers, mainly men."

"Why would anyone volunteer to go to their death?" Anna asked, angry at the situation.

"We don't know that for sure, Anna. Supposedly they need workers to help rebuild cities in Germany that have been damaged by Allied air raids," answered Kwart.

"Allied air raids?" echoed Teddy.

"Yes, Tanchum. The good guys are close," said Kwart. "The Nazis are saying they need men and, if they volunteer, their family will receive more rations."

"I still think we don't volunteer to leave," stated Anna.

"I agree with you, *mine libn*," answered Kwart. "We'll stay here as long as possible; we're safer with what we know."

The Jewish inhabitants of the ghetto had the same mindset. Few people volunteered over the next few days, forcing the Jewish police to go into buildings with lists and collect them.

Kwart came home emotional and disheartened at what he heard and saw day after day.

"I don't know what to believe anymore," said Kwart.

"What's on your mind?" asked Anna.

"We're told to tell the people on the lists that if the men go to these different work camps their family will get more rations. The men will be able to write home and tell them what's going on," said Kwart

"You're not thinking of going, are you?" asked Anna

"No," answered Kwart. "But I don't know what to believe."

Kwart sat down at the kitchen table. Anna rubbed his shoulders, offering any relief she could.

"Is Teddy sleeping?" Kwart asked.

"Yes, why?" responded Anna.

"You don't think the rumors are true, do you?" asked Kwart, turning around to face his wife.

"I'm like you, I don't know what to believe," sighed Anna.

"Could there really be a place created to kill Jews? Where they burn bodies?" Kwart asked nervously.

"It wouldn't surprise me anymore," said Anna, her hands trembling at the thought.

As quickly as they'd started, the deportations stopped.

Nobody knew why. Rumors spread around the ghetto that the Allies were near and their rescue was close. The raids must have done irreparable damage to the Germans' precious cities.

 The thought was short-lived. Two weeks later, deportations began again, this time on a much larger scale.

In order to expedite the process, the SS and German military closed all ghetto factories. No work meant there would not be lunchtime soup. Stomachs already pained from starvation seemed to turn in on themselves.

Rumkowski asked the ghetto inhabitants to remain calm and kindly report for deportation. Nobody listened. Rumors that the Russians were closing in on Lodz made them hide or stay put for as long as possible, clinging to hopes of liberation.

Section by section, the Nazis closed off the ghetto. The Gestapo and armed soldiers searched all buildings in assigned areas. Everyone they found was deported. Once a closed-off section had been entirely searched, it was considered off-limits to everyone. Anyone found in an off-limits area was shot on sight.

The courthouse was closed down at the same time as the factories. Before the doors were locked, Kwart went into the storeroom and opened a box of confiscated jewelry. He took a watch and a few diamond rings, not knowing what the currency would be where they were headed.

Day after day Teddy heard screams getting louder. His effort to keep his mind off the unspeakable horrors going on around him led his thoughts back to his hunger – which was equally unpleasant.

Each day, he stood in the basement staring at the hole covered with aluminum and leaves. He wanted badly to hide, to try to escape everything, but with his family gone what was the point? He had already lost everyone in his life he'd known before the ghetto and did not know if he could take losing everyone in his life since as well.

He trusted Kwart. Together, they would be ok. Teddy made his final trip to the basement thinking about the last memory of his father. He remembered Simcha covering him with the aluminum and leaves now lying on the floor in front of him. He thought about what his father said before the Nazis snatched him away: "Everything has its price." The same phrase he'd used at the ice cream shop to teach Teddy a lesson in a time of innocence had surfaced again in a time of pure evil.

Simcha's life for Teddy's. Wherever Simcha was, dead or alive, he was there so Teddy could live. Teddy took a deep breath and exhaled slowly. He took comfort in knowing that wherever his family was, they were also in his heart following him wherever he went.

He walked up the basement steps for the last time, turning around to stare into the darkness. The scariest place on earth a few years earlier was now a harmless basement, something a small child feared. He'd dealt with far worse in his short fifteen-year lifespan.

The next morning, barking dogs and screams no longer came from other sections of the ghetto. They were coming from Gnieznienska Street. There was no inspection or selection of who stayed and went. Everyone went.

Kwart and his family, including Teddy, did not put up a struggle as they headed outside to join the caravan of people. There was no use in wasting energy for a hopeless cause. They had already packed their suitcases, anticipating this day. They were taking small belongings and clothes, leaving everything else behind.

They pocketed their remaining rations, not knowing when they would next eat, and followed the line north to Marysin and on to Radegast Station. Everyone walking looked equally as bad as they did, some even worse. Emaciated faces peered down at cobblestone streets, trying to comprehend what was happening. Their bodies hungered for food and were barely strong enough to carry their suitcases. The years of extreme hardship and starvation had made them unrecognizable.

As they made their pilgrimage to the train station, it was difficult not to think about the more than one hundred thousand people who had made it before. *What had happened to them? Were they working? Were they alive?*

Teddy reflected on his family and their thoughts when it was their time. *Had Pola been reunited with Touba and Esther before deportation, or had she left separately? Where had the soldiers taken Simcha? Had he gone to the train station or the Red House?* He knew now that Esther had left without Anka and was probably frightened.

Teddy hit himself on the side of the head, cursing under his breath. He'd left Anka at the kitchen table in the apartment. He turned to look behind him but was already too far away to consider going back. He continued walking with the Jewish mass. The doll was just another piece of Teddy's life, lost to the ghetto.

Arriving at the station, Sala could barely stand up. Kwart piled their suitcases on top of each other, creating a makeshift chair for her to sit on. The train had not arrived yet and the crowd grew.

Knowing that concentration camps existed quite nearby, the people wished the train would never come. They'd heard the names of Posnan, Gross-Rosen, and Oswiecim, among others, and had listened to the stories of what happened at the camps, both work and death, forcing themselves to believe they would work. A teenager an earshot away from Teddy mentioned that perhaps the Russians had derailed the train. He wished it were true.

Hopes were dashed at the sound of squealing brakes on the track. Tension rose instantly as everyone watched their fate roll up in front of them. Kwart turned to Teddy, handing him one of the diamond rings he'd taken from the courthouse.

"Put this on, Teddy," said Kwart.

Teddy looked down at the diamond ring as he slipped it on his finger. He faced Kwart, who nodded approvingly. Teddy did not understand why Kwart was giving him the ring but knew it was not the time to question it either.

The train was nothing like Teddy had pictured. Instead of rail cars with windows and seats, a long row of cattle cars pulled up. The color of the wooden boards comprising the sides of the cars resembled the bricks of the Red House – filling Teddy with a terrible sense of dread.

Studying the crowd of frightened people, Teddy figured another train must be coming. There was no way everyone was going to fit on board. He was wrong.

Soldiers placed narrow wooden planks into the openings of the trains. Jews walked the unstable platforms, boarding cars like cattle heading for slaughter. Soldiers with fixed bayonets screamed at those who moved too slowly. Once a car was filled to a capacity the Germans felt appropriate, a soldier sat in the doorway to make sure no one got off.

Teddy, Kwart and his family made their way to the cattle car closest to them. Sala headed up the ramp first. Whilst she was trying to maintain her balance on the narrow board, a soldier pushed her forward. She fell down, but managed to stay on the ramp. Teddy helped her inside. They were the first ones in and headed towards the tiny barred window.

The car was completely bare. It was a gigantic box made from wooden boards. The only thing disrupting its emptiness was a wooden bucket at the opposite end. The smell on board was horrible. Teddy tried figuring out the scent but could not put his finger on what it was.

OK, the car is full enough, Kwart thought to himself. People were already shoulder to shoulder but they continued boarding. Finally, when everyone was jammed tighter than sardines, with barely enough room to lift their arms or bend their knees, the door slammed shut followed by a loud and ominous clunk of the lock.

Thirty minutes later, the train came to life, crawling out of the station. Teddy grabbed the metal grate covering the window and pulled himself up to look outside. It was the first time he'd been out of the ghetto in over four years.

"How long will the trip be, Abba?" asked a thirteen-year-old boy to Teddy's left.

"Depends on where they take us," answered the boy's father. "Hopefully not too long, I can't be in here much longer."

The cramped quarters were enough to drive anyone insane. There was no room to move anywhere. Sitting down was impossible. Teddy breathed deeply to expand his lungs and annoyed the person in front of him by moving too much.

The August temperature was over ninety degrees, putting it well over one hundred in the cattle cars. Body heat radiating off everyone made the already suffocating conditions worse. A man behind Kwart continually breathed on his neck. The sensation of his breath made Kwart feel like his skin was burning off.

Teddy realized, as did many others, the intention of the wooden bucket at the opposite end of the cart. It was the toilet. With the amount of people jammed into the confines of the box, it was impossible for anyone to use it unless they stood next to it. Everyone faced two choices: hold it, or go where they stood.

Teddy pulled himself back up to the window for some fresh air. Looking outside, he decided to give descriptions of what he saw, trying to brighten everyone's spirits. He painted vivid pictures in their minds with his imagery. Teddy spoke of birds flying freely wherever they pleased. Cows stood in open pastures with no fences confining them.

Seeing nobody was interested, Teddy dropped down to the floor and stayed quiet. They were five hours into the trip, with no end in sight. Teddy reached into his pocket and pulled out a small chunk of bread he'd packed before leaving and ate it.

The few people close to the bucket were lucky enough to use it. Everyone else relieved themselves where they stood. The smell was nauseating and getting worse as it combined with the intense heat. As time went on and more people urinated and defecated, the conditions became unbearable and inhumane.

As the sun began to set, everyone prepared for a sleepless night. With no place to sit, they all stood. Teddy and Sala took turns sleeping. First Sala rested her head on Teddy's shoulders, then, when she awoke, they switched. There was no relief from the heat after the sun set as Teddy had hoped, leaving him realizing there was no reprieve for them except getting off the train.

Conditions worsened the following morning. The smell became so horrific that people could barely hold back from vomiting. Those unable to overcome the urge threw up on people unlucky enough to be in the way.

Those without food panicked, not knowing whether or when they would eat again. And regardless of food, everyone ached for water. There was none on board and all needed it. The heat dehydrated them to the brink of hallucination. Teddy kept his mouth shut, holding moisture in, but could not handle the smell from breathing though his nose. He opened it occasionally, escaping the awful odor plaguing the railcar.

Sala coughed uncontrollably. The dryness in her throat left nothing to combat the typhus she was battling. She tried her best to cough downwards to keep her breath from burning everyone around her.

The extended length of time Sala stood weighed heavily on her. Her knees buckled, intermittently giving out underneath her. She caught herself a few times on Teddy and Rebekah. As dehydration sunk deeper, she began mumbling her words and not making sense.

Teddy reached into his pocket for the last piece of bread he had. With no idea of how much longer they would have to endure this nightmare, he took the gamble and placed it in his mouth. He sucked on it for a while, stimulating saliva production, then swallowed.

People prayed while others broke down in tears. Teddy continued lifting himself to the window for fresh air, mentally escaping the madness inside. People asked if he saw any signs to get bearings on where they headed, but he did not see any.

That night, Sala stopped coughing. She looked peaceful as she laid her head on Teddy's shoulder. Teddy looked at the starry night through the window. It was the first time in years he could remember looking at stars.

Besides occasional moaning, terrible joint aches from standing so long and the horrific smells of feces, urine and vomit, the night felt calm. The rhythmic sound of the train on its track helped remove Teddy from his surroundings.

He reflected on his family. Had they gone through this as well? What had they been thinking? He thought about Esther. How brave she was to go through it without Anka.

The splatter on the floor behind him snapped Teddy out of his dream and into a gagging fit as he felt whatever had hit the floor spread over his legs.

He must have fallen into a deep sleep while thinking about his family. The sun shone brightly through the window and into Teddy's eyes. Unable to move his body to get away from the glare, he turned his head to the right.

Sala still lay on his shoulder, but she was no longer there. She had died during the night. Her mouth and eyes were open wide but she appeared peaceful. She no longer suffered.

"Kwart," said Teddy, gently pulling at his shirt.

Kwart looked over his shoulder at Teddy and saw Sala. He nudged Anna, pointing back to her mother. Rebekah was already aware her mother had passed.

Two years ago, when the family thought they'd lost Sala during the hospital liquidation, everyone had cried. Now it was accepted. They all knew things were not getting better and her death at that moment was better than what was coming. Slowly and respectfully, Rebekah reached into her mother's pocket. She pulled out her remaining bread and divided it equally between them.

A group of people on the other side of the train began crying. They too had lost a family member. Four additional people died during the day, bringing a concentrated hysteria to the cattle car.

"They're not going to stop the train until we're all dead!" shouted a woman.

"We're going to cook in here," yelled someone else.

Unable to deal with everything going on in the cattle car, Teddy lifted himself up to look out the window. He saw farmers tending their crops and children running with the train.

One boy stood still with an evil smile on his face. He raised his hand up to his neck and, using his pointer finger, slowly made a throat-slitting motion. Taken aback, Teddy looked away, shaking off what he'd seen. He dropped down from the window appalled, keeping quiet as he did not want to scare anyone.

As the sun set for the third time, conditions were at their worst. Everywhere Teddy stepped landed him in feces. It was a chore to breathe. The extremely cramped quarters and smell made him want to hold his breath indefinitely.

"Tanchum, help me," said Anna.

She reached down to the floor, trying to pull Sala's shoes off. Teddy leaned over and pulled at one. They struggled, eventually getting them off. They were women's shoes with a heel lift.

"Put these on, Tanchum," said Anna. "They'll make you look taller."

Teddy did not understand why he needed to look taller but he did not question her. He navigated his leg up through the mass of people and took off his boot. Too big for him, the boots belonging to his father came off with ease.

He proceeded to put on Sala's shoes, which were too small for him. After five minutes, Teddy managed to put on both of Sala's shoes, only breaking the buckle on one, and then slipped his feet back into Simcha's boots.

Anna was right; Teddy was taller. He was a good three inches higher than before but the view remained the same. People confined to their tiny spaces, starving, unable to breath, covered in urine and feces.

Exhausted from the energy expended putting on Sala's shoes, Teddy rested his head on the wooden wall of the cattle car and shut his eyes.

The familiar squealing of the train braking bolted Teddy awake. It was dark outside. He guessed around three in the morning. The relief of finally getting off the train and anxiety at dealing with their fate pumped adrenaline through everyone's veins.

A few people screamed. Others began to cry. Members of families who could not wait to move around separate from one another now clung together.

The lock clunked free of its grasp on the hatch. The doors viciously slid open on screaming hinges. Fresh air rushed into the stagnant compartment while lights pointing at the train blinded its victims.

A man eagerly walked up the ramp and stood in the doorway. He appeared as a towering black mass silhouetted by the light behind him. Teddy thought the only thing making him more menacing would be his eyes glowing red.

The man did not introduce himself, nor did he give orders. He just yelled, "*Raus, Schnell.*"

#

15: Awakening To a Nightmare

Like a well-oiled machine, the Germans created a scene of complete yet organized chaos in minutes. Two additional SS members came up and began throwing people to the ramp below.

The man in front of Teddy, and who appeared to be on the verge of death, shuffled forward to get off the train. A soldier hit him in the head with the butt of his rifle. As he dropped dead to the edge of the train car, the soldier kicked him the rest of the way like garbage.

Teddy stayed by Kwart's side. He looked back at Sala's body, thankful she was not alive. This was a far worse place.

Everyone moved hastily, leaving their suitcases behind them. Teddy trembled with fear as his eyes focused on the pandemonium in front of him.

The area smelled foul, like burnt rubber and something else he could not place. Rows of barbed wire fences surrounded everything. Guard towers housed machine guns, aimed at the new arrivals. In the near distance were chimneys from which flames and smoke blasted like furious dragons. Brick and wooden barracks lined up in rows of flawless harmony to house countless numbers of prisoners, of slaves, of Jews.

Hateful soldiers with barking dogs met them. The German Shepherds and Doberman Pincers were the scariest dogs Teddy had ever seen. They foamed angrily at their mouths lined with razor sharp teeth. Each time one barked, Teddy instinctively jumped in terror.

The Germans moved swiftly, not giving anyone time to think. They began separating the men from the women. As families were torn apart, mothers held on to their boys until the last possible second. Fathers cried as they watched their daughters being dragged away.

Kwart saw this happening with a heavy heart. He grabbed Anna, giving her a long hug and kiss. He then faced Rebekah, telling her to take care of his wife.

Once they were pulled apart, Anna and Rebekah followed one line while Kwart and Teddy were led to another. Teddy and Kwart spoke German and understood everything the soldiers said. They followed orders to blend in and not stand out too much.

Approaching the head of the line, Teddy focused on the scene in front of him. It appeared that the SS utilized the same method as the soldiers organizing the deportation that had taken his family. The sick, young and elderly went in one direction while the healthy went another. Teddy assumed the only way to better the odds, much like in Lodz, was to look healthy and work. He noticed a huge difference in people going one direction versus the other.

He pinched both cheeks, like his mother had done before the deportation selection. Twelve men ahead of them went to the left with the sick, young and elderly.

Kwart approached the head of the line. In front of him sat a handsome, clean-cut doctor wearing the whitest of gloves and holding a horse-riding crop in his right hand.

"What can you do?" the doctor asked.

"I'm a plumber, carpenter and locksmith," replied Kwart.

At that moment, Teddy heard Simcha whisper in his ear, "Stand up straight, *mine yingl*." Teddy, caught off guard, turned around hoping to see his father but instead locked eyes with a nervous stranger from the train.

The doctor sitting in front of Kwart gestured right with his riding crop towards the strong and healthy. Teddy stepped up next. He firmly planted his feet, standing as tall as his starving body allowed.

Before the doctor asked him the same question, he answered.

"I can do everything you need, I'm a locksmith too," said Teddy confidently in German.

The doctor studied the boy standing in front of him. Teddy showed poise but was panicking within. He stared straight ahead, frightened to make eye contact with his fate. After a long moment, the doctor lifted his riding crop and motioned to the right.

Teddy exhaled, relieved to see which direction he'd been sent in. He walked over and stood behind Kwart. They hugged, happy to be reunited, but still had no idea what was happening. Kwart scanned the women's line behind them, searching for Anna and Rebekah. They were nowhere in sight, lost in a crowd of thousands. He prayed they were together and safe.

The handful of men deemed healthy marched into a large brick building where they undressed and removed any valuables they possessed. Eleven wedding bands and six watches were collected. The men had sold everything valuable they owned years earlier for food in the ghetto. Kwart gave up the jewelry he'd stolen from the courthouse. Teddy took the ring Kwart gave him and clenched it tightly in his fist, not wanting it confiscated.

The men walked single file to another room. Seven at a time, they stood on stools in front of the new arrivals while prisoners of the camp completely shaved them from head to toe.

As Teddy stepped onto the stool, his body trembled. The lack of food was catching up with him. The prisoner shaving his hair hummed an unfamiliar tune. *What are you so happy about*? Teddy thought, looking down at the man, who was himself devoid of all body hair.

Teddy stepped off the stool, looking identical to everyone else. Without hair or clothes, it became difficult to tell each other apart. Nevertheless, Kwart recognized Teddy and called him over.

"Move, quickly!" yelled an SS officer standing next to an exit.

Everyone picked up their pace, running naked into a new room filled with barrels of liquid that reeked unlike anything they had smelled before. They all sat obediently in the barrels, which turned out to be filled with disinfectant, designed to get rid of vermin they might have brought into the camp. Teddy was shorter than everyone else in the group. Sitting in the disinfectant barrel, he held his breath to prevent the liquid from entering his mouth.

A handful of powder hit Teddy's face while climbing out the vile liquid, temporarily blinding him. As he slowly regained his eyesight, the powder hit him a few more times, burning his skin.

"Make it quick!" another SS officer yelled.

Teddy and Kwart continued to follow the other prisoners as the group moved into a large room with showerheads. The doors slammed shut behind them, and was locked from the outside. The men stood silent as they wondered what would happen next.

Suddenly, boiling water erupted out of the showerheads. The men cried out in surprise and pain, pushing each other out of the way to escape the scalding downpour. Kwart fell to the floor, trampled by the horde that ran to the door to plead for help. The water eventually stopped and prisoners backed away from the door, returning to the center of the room.

Without any more warning than the last time, freezing water began to pour from the showerheads, causing panic to return. Everyone again ran for the door, desperate to escape the torrent. When the cold water finally stopped, slightly warmer water dripped for thirty seconds. By the time the ordeal ended, most men still had disinfectant on them, too afraid to go under the water to wash it off.

A metal door on the far side of the room swung open, slamming into the cement wall behind it with a deafening sound.

"Hurry up," yelled another officer.

The half-showered men emptied the room quickly. They ran outside, soaking wet, before heading into another part of the building. The new prisoners entered an area where old inmates threw clothes at them across tables. Pants, shirts, hats, all different sizes but sporting the same striped pattern, flew everywhere. Teddy picked up a pair of pants that fit him perfectly, but the shirt he had chosen hung off his small body, several sizes too large. He traded it with a man whose shirt was several sizes too small. The top was still big, but better than the original one.

Another SS officer screamed. Teddy and Kwart, dressed in their prison garb, ran through the door and outside. They marched through the camp towards the barracks.

"What's going on?" Teddy asked Kwart.

"I have no idea," Kwart answered.

The new inmates saw men in striped uniforms matching the ones they now wore through barbed wire fences. These prisoners were moving bricks, digging holes and shoveling sand though their emaciated bodies hardly looked sturdy enough to keep them standing on their feet. Teddy wondered if he had enough energy to do anything that strenuous.

Rows of wooden stable-like barracks stood to the left and right of Teddy as he walked down the path between them. The walls were completely solid with no windows. Instead, a long row of skylights sprawled across the entire length of the roofs.

As the group of newcomers walked along, soldiers chose men to go into them. They would later learn the camp was called Auschwitz. They selected Kwart for one barrack while Teddy was pressed forward. The two said goodbye with their eyes. Teddy walked on, making a note of which building Kwart had disappeared into. He wanted to be sure he could return and check in on his friend to see if he was still alive.

The remaining prisoners were the youngest of the bunch. They were the children who had survived the *Gehsperre* in Lodz and appeared the strongest during earlier selections. Teddy recognized one of the boys. His name was Abraham and he was a year younger than Teddy. Everyone else was a new face. They came to barracks number 11 and walked inside.

From the look of things, it appeared to be a children's barracks. The hundreds of kids ranged between nine and eighteen years old. Most were close to death. They were filthy, no more than skin and bones, muscles wasted away.

The inside of the barracks smelled damp and moldy. Rows of wooden bunks stacked three levels high lined both sides of the walls. A chimney was on either side of the room with a brick duct running the room's length. There were no windows and no air circulation.

Teddy headed down the barracks and found an empty bed on the middle bunk to claim as his own. Abraham picked the spot next to him and said hello. They had never spoken to each other in school, but now they were all each other had. Teddy nodded back.

As he went to sit down on the bunk's edge, he noticed something hard pressing against the side of his leg. Teddy stood up, curious to see what it was. Guardedly, he reached into the pocket and pulled out a piece of pork.

He had no idea how long the pork had been there and did not want to know what had happened to its previous owner. Quickly, he jammed the pork back into his pocket and looked around to see if anyone noticed. In the confusion caused by the new arrivals, nobody had seen anything. The hard pork rubbed against his skinny leg and begged Teddy to eat it. He tamped down the urge, making a deal with himself to eat no more than a sliver a day to make it last as long as possible.

That night, Teddy lay in his tiny bunk with Abraham and three other kids. They wedged together on their sides for everyone to fit. Longing for their parents, a few of the younger children's cries broke the silence.

Teddy ignored them. He wanted to roll over and shut his eyes but there was no room to move. Those crying had only just been separated from their families. Teddy had been without his for two years.

What he could not ignore were the stories. Some of the older kids took it upon themselves to inform the children where their families were.

"Shut up already. They're gone," said one boy.

"They've gone up the chimney," said another.

"What do you mean, they've gone up the chimney?" asked one of the new arrivals.

An eighteen year old whispered the horrors of what happened to those who had gone to the left instead of the right.

"First the soldiers lead them to the woods to sit," he started. "They then march them into a room to be shaved like we are," he continued. The entire room was silent as the teenager captured everyone's attention. "Next, they tell them they're going to wash and bring them into a shower room," he went on, "but instead of water, poisonous gas comes from the showerheads and kills them all. Then they're burned in big ovens so that they don't have to waste time and energy burying them."

"That's not true," whined a newcomer, unwilling to believe the story.

"It is true," another boy chimed in. "That awful smell around the camp is burning hair and skin. We probably smell the people you were transported with right now."

Everyone knew deep down that the stories were true. The thought of how many people had already been gassed and burned made Teddy feel nauseous. He tried hard to clear his mind, though he could not help but wonder if Anna and Rebekah had been sent left or right. *Were they together or apart? Did he smell them now?* He thought about his family, their once strong bodies shrunken and weak from the harsh conditions of the ghetto. *What would their fates have been in this miserable and frightening place?*

Stuck on his side, unable to roll and exhausted from the day, Teddy shut his eyes and fell into a deep sleep. He woke up a few times, suffocating from the intense body heat and poor air circulation around him.

Early in the morning, a loud bell went off and the doors to the children's barracks flew open. The *kapo* walked into the overheated room, screaming for the young prisoners to get up. The man was only a few years older than the children were, but he marched in with an air of extraordinary power. He must have been selected *kapo* of children's barracks 11 because he appeared so young. It was a position of extreme power on a tiny level and he took full advantage.

Most of the children were new to Auschwitz-Birkenau, the largest of the three Auschwitz camps. They had not expected to rise so early in the morning. They were still groggy, and got to their feet with joints achy from sleeping on wooden bunks.

"Line up!" yelled the *kapo*.

Teddy stood at attention next to Abraham. A young boy on the opposite side of the room a few bunks down was mortified at the sight of the *kapo*. He lost control of his bladder, urinating in his pants. Without saying a word, the *kapo* walked up to him and took a swing. The punch landed on the boy's cheek, sending him to the ground.

"No one pees on my floor unless I say so," yelled the *kapo*.

The boy stood back up at attention, his cheek already beginning to swell. He swayed from side to side, dizzy from the punch. The two adjacent boys steadied him.

"This is Birkenau," commanded the *kapo*. "Work hard and you may live long enough to die later."

The kapo stopped in the center of the room and pointed upward.

"See this beam on the ceiling? Whoever does not hand over any gold, diamonds or money that any of you conniving Jews have smuggled in will be hanged from it."

The *kapo* paced up and down the aisle staring angrily at each child, seeing if they had valuables on them they had not handed over after the initial selection.

Teddy cautiously took off his ring and placed it in his pocket next to the pork. He did not want to give it up and was sure he could keep it hidden.

The *kapo* walked past Teddy and Abraham, paying them no attention. When he reached the end of the line, he turned around and exited the barracks, leaving the young prisoners to think about his threat.

Prisoners entered the barracks carrying breakfast. Teddy received half a liter of something resembling coffee and a piece of weeks-old black bread. Looking around, he observed that most of the new arrivals ate the entire piece of bread, while the more experienced kids ate a small portion before putting the rest in their pockets.

Teddy sipped his coffee, gagging at its bitterness. He took pleasure from the fact it was hot and the first thing he had ingested since arriving. He managed to get the rest down with relative ease. He took a small bite of bread before putting the rest in his pocket next to the piece of pork.

Another bell sounded and the *kapo* returned, yelling again. This time he ordered the prisoners to line up outside the barracks in rows of five. Everyone was eager to obey and they ran as fast as their bodies could carry them. He inspected the rows, screaming at kids to stand straight. If a child was not standing tall enough, or their feet were not exactly a shoulder's width apart from his neighbor's, the *kapo* beat them while yelling at them to stand upright. When he decided everyone was presentable, he ordered them to work detail.

The group broke out into a quick jog to the fields they had passed the previous day. There, they were responsible for moving bricks from one section of the field to the other. The task seemed simple at first, but the lack of food drained the children's energy quickly, causing their joints to scream in agony.

In the background, the chimneys blasted smoke. The sight of them reminded Teddy of the older boy's story of what those chimneys really were. His stomach clenched in fear. The smoke covered everything and the smell was impossible to escape. In some strange way, the boy's story made sense to Teddy. Trains never stopped arriving, the same way the chimneys never stopped smoking. Cruel images entered his mind about people smelling him one day.

Through the barbed wire fences, Teddy saw another work detail. Men dug a long narrow hole. One of them, who had been struggling to lift his shovel, sat down to rest his tired body. Before he had reached the ground, one of the SS shot him dead. Experienced prisoners did not jump at the gunshot. It happened every day. Two inmates dragged the dead prisoner away to the ovens.

Abraham's body began breaking down halfway through the day. His stomach churned angrily with hunger. He went to sit down to relieve his pains.

"Don't," whispered Teddy.

"I need to, I'm so tired," Abraham whispered back.

"It'll be the chimney if you do," responded Teddy, nudging his head for Abraham to look through the barbed wire. Abraham stood back up.

After a long, grueling day, the boys were eager for sustenance, though they knew better than to hope for a satisfying meal. They marched back to the barracks, where they received no more than a bit of cheese spread. First-timers looked around in confusion, unsure of whether anything else would come. As the realization that they had squandered their bread ration at breakfast dawned, they began to sob, resigning themselves to satisfy their unhappy stomachs with the meager portion of cheese.

Teddy reached into his pocket and took out his piece of bread. Looking around to ensure no one was watching, he grabbed the piece of pork and pulled off a thin chunk. He placed the pork on the bread, covered it with the cheese, and ate his dinner.

After their meal, the prisoners were allowed to walk around their barracks. Teddy made his way to the building Kwart had disappeared into, hoping he would find him safely inside.

"Tanchum!" exclaimed Kwart, excited to see his friend was alive.

It was only their second day in the camp, but it felt like a lifetime since they had seen one another. Kwart introduced Teddy to a few of the men from his barracks. Teddy recognized four of them from the train.

Teddy brought up the chimney story from the previous night and Kwart confirmed that he had heard the same thing. They prayed together that Anna and Rebekah had made it through selections.

The bell sounded. Like clockwork, everyone parted ways, heading back to their own barracks for the night. Teddy was on his way back to barracks 11 when he felt a heavy hand settle on his shoulder. A voice whispered, "Stay," and Teddy could have sworn that the voice belonged to his father. He spun around, but Simcha was nowhere to be seen. Teddy looked up at Kwart, a feeling of dread welling up inside of him.

"I don't want to go back to my barracks," he said.

"You have to," answered Kwart.

"I can't. Can I stay with you?" asked Teddy.

Kwart could not bring himself to deny the frightened face of the boy he had promised to take care of.

"I'll leave that up to you, Tanchum, but if you stay, you'll need to make it back to your barracks before the morning bell. Who knows what will happen to us if they catch you," said Kwart.

Teddy relaxed visibly and followed Kwart back into his barracks.

The sleeping conditions were the same as the children's barracks: extremely hot and poorly ventilated. A few rats scurried around the floor, their claws skittering quickly across the wooden boards. Most men could not stop itching from the lice now permanently residing on their bodies.

Teddy climbed up to the third level bunk and lay down next to Kwart. He could feel the pork sandwiched between his leg and the wooden platform. It was uncomfortable to lie on but Teddy did not mind. It let him know he was still alive.

He awoke early in the morning, knowing he needed to return to the children's barracks before the bell rang. He struggled to get out of the bunk, trying not to disturb Kwart and their bedmates and not put too much strain on his aching muscles.

Once freed, he carefully lowered himself down. Quietly, he crept down the long center isle of the barracks. When he came to the door at the end, he cracked it open and peeked outside.

A strong whiff of chimney smoke hit Teddy in the face. *There must have been another train*, he thought to himself, shaking his head in fear and disgust.

Seeing the path was clear of Germans, he left Kwart's barracks and made his way to his own. Staying close to walls of the buildings and keeping to the shadows, Teddy kept his ears open for guards, making sure to keep his footsteps as quiet as possible.

He approached barracks 11 without incident, guessing he had a few minutes before the bell rang. Letting out a sigh of relief, Teddy cracked the door open and snuck inside.

He shut the door behind him and froze, trying to comprehend the sight before him. Something was terribly wrong. The children's barracks was empty.

#

16: Luck

Teddy did not know what to do. *Where is everyone?* he thought. He wanted to crawl into a corner and hide, but knew he could not stay in the barracks. If the SS came in there and found him, they would kill him.

He hurried through to the other end, seeing if it was truly empty or if anyone was still hiding. No one was there. He rested his hand on the bottom of the wooden bunk. It was still warm. Whatever had happened to everyone had happened recently.

Abraham. The name echoed through Teddy's head. *What's going on?* he wondered. Teddy played scenarios in his mind about what Abraham must have experienced as the children left the barracks. *Did he know what was going to happen?*

Not knowing how much time remained before the bell sounded, Teddy decided he needed to act quickly so he made his way back to Kwart's barracks. Peeking out of the children's barracks, he saw the path was clear. The smell of chimney smoke brought unwelcome visions of children screaming for their mothers. He banished the sight from his mind and followed the route he'd taken moments earlier, this time in reverse.

Teddy was three barracks away. He peeked around the final corner, hoping he was home free, but much to his dismay two guards were walking in his direction. He concealed himself in the darkness and luckily went unnoticed. He heard their boots on the dirt walkway coming closer. Teddy took a few steps back to ensure they would not be able to see him.

The guards laughed and casually conversed about finding the victims of gas chambers in awkward positions when the doors were opened: mothers clutching on to their children, people piled on top of each other by the door, clawing to get out. An elderly man had stood leaning forward with his head balancing on the wall, his arms hanging lifelessly down in front of him, his entire body covered in black and blue from the poisonous gas.

The visual descriptions, coupled with the grotesque smell of chimney smoke, made Teddy nauseous. He held his breath as the soldiers walked by his hiding spot between the barracks. Once they'd passed he let out a sigh of relief. They continued walking, their laughs echoing in the distance.

With no one else in sight, Teddy crept silently into Kwart's barracks. He crawled up to the bunk to lie back down but there was no space for him. He tapped Kwart's leg to wake him up.

"What are you still doing here?" whispered Kwart.

"My barracks is empty," replied Teddy. "I can't go back there."

"What do you mean, empty?" asked Kwart.

"I don't know. There was nobody in it," answered Teddy.

Kwart shifted over as much as he could for Teddy to lie down. Five minutes later the bell went off.

Immediately, the *kapo* of Kwart's barracks yelled, "Up, up, *schnell*."

Everyone was now familiar with the routine and began moving. Teddy realized he needed to learn quickly in Birkenau otherwise he could be punished, or worse.

He got up, blending in with other prisoners. He was the youngest by about four years and a few inches shorter than everyone else was. However, most men had been in the camp for a while and had lost a lot of muscle mass, which made Teddy look stronger.

Everyone received a piece of old bread and terrible coffee. Teddy took a few bites before saving the rest in his pocket with the pork. The men were ordered to line up outside before reporting to their designated area for labor.

The *kapo* paced in front of the prisoners, counting them. Teddy's heart raced as the *kapo* looked at him while he was passing by.

Two soldiers approached the *kapo*, who proceeded to tell them that something was wrong with the count. Teddy almost blacked out hearing the *kapo*'s words. The soldiers fixed bayonets and marched towards him. Teddy made eye contact with the *kapo* as the guards strode up.

He prepared himself for the worst, shutting his eyes and bracing himself for the impact. The footsteps got louder, but nothing happened. He opened his eyes to see the guards go past him into the barracks. Screams reverberated within, as bayonets impaled those too weak to get out of bed or work. An eerie silence followed the guards exiting the barracks. They were wiping their bloody bayonets clean on a few of the prisoners' garbs.

The *kapo* pointed to Teddy and three other men, telling them to go into the barracks and remove the bodies. Without question, Teddy followed orders, elated that he had not been discovered. *Not yet at least*, he thought.

Inside the barracks, Teddy counted eight dead bodies. He figured five must have died during the night. Their uniforms were free of blood and their bodies cold. The other three had definitely been alive a few moments earlier. Two bodies had several puncture wounds in their chests while the third had one through his neck.

Teddy gagged at the thought of removing the bodies. He'd become accustomed to seeing them for years but, apart from Sala, these were the first he'd touched.

The three men began going through the pockets of the dead, searching for food. Four of the bodies had pieces of bread in their pockets, which the three men and Teddy split. Teddy thought about how lucky a person would be finding the pork in his pocket.

The men who had died during the night were frightfully light to carry compared to those who'd been murdered. Their bones shone through their skin.

"*Muselmann*," said the man helping Teddy carry a body, pointing at the corpse with his chin.

It was the term for the walking dead around camp – those people succumbing to starvation and exhaustion and not having much longer to live.

Once Teddy had pulled the last body free of the barracks, he turned to see a wagon piled heavy with death. He cringed, sensing the truck's open gate begging for more corpses. Twenty bodies of those who either had not survived the night or had been murdered in the morning already crowded the truck from other barracks.

After loading the bodies, the men reported to their work detail to move countless bricks across fields and try to live another day. Teddy overheard a few men whispering about trucks coming in the middle of the night to cart the occupants of the children's barracks to the gas chambers. His mind reflected on Abraham and the crying children.

During evening roll call, the *kapo* pointed to two of the men who'd been loading dead bodies onto the trucks. He told them to hurry to the front.

When they arrived, the *kapo* sent the faster one back into line. The slower man, explained the *kapo*, had been seen taking food from the dead bodies that morning and needed to be punished.

Teddy and the other men knew no one had seen them take food. The *kapo* made everything up to use as an example to other prisoners. However, they also knew that if they spoke up, whatever was about to happen to their accomplice would happen to them as well. They all kept quiet.

The *kapo* punched the inmate in the stomach, leaving him hunched over and struggling to breathe. Then he took out a whip and began lashing into the man, making him count the strokes in German.

Teddy put his head down unable to stomach the agonizing cries. An SS officer walked up to him and lifted his head, forcing him to watch.

After the flogging, the men went inside to receive their supper. Teddy ripped off another piece of pork. He made his meager sandwich and ate it quietly before climbing to the top bunk. The cries of pain coming from the inmate who'd been beaten kept everyone awake through the night.

Towards the end of the first week, hunger totally overwhelmed Teddy. He bravely approached his *kapo* at suppertime to tell him that he'd found a diamond ring while laboring in hopes of trading it for extra food. He pulled the ring out of his pocket to show to the *kapo*. After examining it, the *kapo* placed the ring in his pocket and told Teddy to be last in line for breakfast the next morning. Teddy nodded and walked away.

The next morning, after the other prisoners had received their breakfast, Teddy walked up for his. The *kapo* reached into his shirt and took out a large piece of bread and handed it to him. Teddy immediately broke the bread in half. He ate a quarter of it before putting the other piece in his pocket. He then gave Kwart the other half of bread, explaining how he got it. Kwart thanked Teddy appreciatively and stuffed the bread into his pocket.

After a few weeks, Teddy felt the full effects of what Auschwitz-Birkenau was doing to him and everyone around him. Death was everywhere. The air he breathed was a constant reminder. A day would not go by without seeing multiple murders and it weighed heavily on him. He was indifferent about death but could not understand how the Germans delivered it so easily all day long, even laughing about it.

Teddy's preoccupied mind did not let him realize he'd stopped while carrying bricks to stare at an SS guard beat a prisoner a few hundred yards away. The man behind Teddy shoved him forward so he would not get into trouble. Teddy put his head down and picked up his pace, but it was too late. A guard had seen the push.

Angered that a Jew had nudged another prisoner without his permission, the SS officer stomped over to Teddy and the man behind him. He grabbed their striped shirts and yanked them over to the center of the field, where he made them stand shoulder to shoulder. The guard announced to everyone in the immediate vicinity to stand around and stare at Teddy and the other man. He grabbed a random individual from the group of onlookers, and placed him next to Teddy.

The German marched around the three men, lecturing the spectators on the repercussions of putting their hands on anyone else without permission from higher authorities.

Without wavering, the officer pulled his pistol out and fired it into the genitals of the man he'd picked at random. The man dropped to his knees, clutching his wound, before falling to the ground and rolling onto his back.

After a few seconds, the man felt no pain. He stopped quivering and stared at the sky, finding comfort in knowing he would shortly leave hell on earth and be reunited with his family who had already died.

The shot fired into his head confirmed his thoughts. Teddy and the man who'd pushed him were sent back to work, making sure not to draw additional attention to themselves. They would not be lucky enough to get away with their lives twice.

After labor, Teddy and Kwart carried the dead prisoner away. Some of their colleagues carried the bodies of others who'd died during labor, through the physical stress and malnourishment of life in Birkenau, and murder.

That night, Teddy finished his final piece of pork. As small as it was, he'd made good on his promise to himself by making it last twenty-four days. Instead of making a sandwich with it, he placed the pork into his mouth and sucked on it for ten minutes to get as much out of it as he could. When it was gone, he ate his bread before climbing into his bunk to lie down.

Not having the pork press on Teddy's leg as he lay on his side was a strange feeling, giving him the sensation that he had lost yet another thing in his life. But at least he'd controlled the pork's fate.

The next morning, the prisoners lined up before reporting to labor. Three guards and an officer came to the line-up as they did every day. The officer paced through the ranks of inmates, casually pointing to a few who did not look well enough to work. A soldier grabbed the people he pointed to and escorted them to the front of the line-up. When the rest of the barracks headed to labor detail, the thirty men selected went off in the other direction, to the gas chambers.

At lunchtime, a few prisoners went past carrying large metal tins filled with lukewarm soup. It consisted of warm water thickened by potato peelings, beets, rutabaga, rye flour and a few grouts.

"Maybe there will be a rat in it this time!" an inmate joked.

"We should only be so lucky," said another.

Teddy used the same philosophy he'd learned in the ghetto. He stayed towards the back of the line while other men fought to be first. He hoped for thicker soup down at the bottom. His thinking paid off, though it was not by much.

In bad shape, Teddy's body had broken down from lack of food. His muscles were not responding as he wanted. The *kapo* saw this and came over to him. He told Teddy to be last in line for supper. Knowing what this meant, Teddy agreed.

After everyone received soup, he approached the *kapo* who let Teddy clean out the bottom of the pot. It was the thickest soup he had eaten in years. He smiled appreciatively before walking to his bunk for the night.

Two weeks later, while moving bricks Teddy noticed a guard pointing his rifle at various inmates, including himself, as they worked. He tried not to let on what he'd seen, fearing the soldier would shoot him.

After twenty minutes, the soldier fired a single shot and dropped two prisoners. Another guard walked up, shaking his hand and passing him a pack of cigarettes as if he'd lost a bet. After seeing guards gambling on human life, Teddy resigned himself to the fact that the only way out of Birkenau was through the chimney.

The cruelty of the guards had no limits. Teddy permanently feared for his life, always reminded of its value to the Germans by the constant smells of burning flesh and hair. Evening roll calls lasted for hours and usually included a form of torture for inmates to witness. Floggings occurred daily. Most times, the prisoners receiving their lashings were forced to keep count in German. More often than not, they lost count due to the intense pain and needed to start over.

 If a prisoner was unable to stand for the entire roll call, guards escorted him away to the gas chamber. Men were no longer men. They were numbers working their hardest to avoid the inevitable.

The *kapo* of Teddy's barracks took a liking to him and placed him in a group of five prisoners charged with delivering bread to the barracks. Four men pushed the wagon while Teddy steered. One day he saw another group of men pushing a similar wagon. The man who was steering crawled underneath and pulled a few pieces of bread through gaps in the floor.

Teddy studied the floor of his wagon, identifying a few spaces wide enough to pull bread through. He ducked under, reaching into the gaps and pulling six chunks out through the bottom. He shared his bounty with the men he was working with and put one piece in his pocket for Kwart.

The next day, Teddy saw the same man crawl under the wagon he was steering. Teddy prepared himself to go underneath his wagon when one of the others pushed him to tell him to wait. Teddy looked up to see if anyone was around. He gazed over at the other wagon and saw a German standing there. The five men watched the SS officer beat the bread thief to death. Teddy voluntarily went back to moving bricks the following morning.

It had been six weeks since Teddy and Kwart had arrived in Auschwitz. Their barracks held approximately seven hundred men. Only a handful of the people who'd arrived with them were still living.

The bite in the air told Teddy it was October. The thin layer of striped prison garb did nothing to warm his thin, starving body. As he did every day, Teddy spent the day moving bricks, keeping a brisk pace to show no weakness. In the distance, inmates heard gunfire and explosions. Everyone looked in the direction of the noise trying to see something, anything.

"Maybe it's the Russians," said one prisoner.

"God, I hope so," answered another.

"It's so close," observed someone else.

The better-informed guards watching over the prisoners knew it was not coming from the Russians. Kwart could tell from their faces that they did not know what was going on either. Whatever was happening was a surprise.

 After work, the men made their thirty-minute trek back to Birkenau, their minds frantically wondering what they would see on arrival.

Approaching the camp, smoke billowed out of crematorium IV as usual, but the smoke was different. The smell in the air was different. It was not only coming out of the chimney but out of the walls.

Contrary to what everyone had hoped, the Russians were not there but the increased SS presence confirmed something had gone down. Upon entering camp, everyone marched quickly to their barracks. They were told to keep their heads down and not look around.

That evening, the prisoners lined up for four hours. The chill in the air made their starving bodies ache. Everyone wondered what the repercussions would be for whatever had happened earlier. Someone would have to pay, and they all knew it would be them.

After hours of standing, the prisoners entered their barracks, ate quickly, and got ready for bed. Rumors circulated about the explosion being an inside job. Other inmates speculated a malfunction in the crematorium had caused the explosion. In the back of everyone's minds was the fact that it did not matter how it had happened: the Jews were to blame.

The next morning, everything appeared routine except for the rising smoke from the crematorium. Soldiers with fixed bayonets ran into barracks to impale men too weak to stand. Prisoners were heard screaming before a deafening silence and the eventual re-emergence of the guards. It was business as usual before labor detail, but also somehow not.

An SS officer paced back and forth pointing at prisoners who looked strong enough to stand but unable to work. As usual the men were collected and sent off to the gas chamber. But that was where the routine changed.

Another SS officer stood in front of the prisoners. Teddy peered at him without making eye contact. He had not seen this officer in camp before. His freshly-pressed uniform was without a speck of dirt. His boots were blindingly shiny.

He paced around the prisoners like the other officer had done before him. He joyfully walked between them, holding his hands behind him and humming a playful tune. The officer tapped Berkowicz on the shoulder. Berkowicz was one of the newest men placed in the barracks and the healthiest one of the group. A soldier escorted him to the front of the line-up.

Teddy visualized the SS making an example out of him, and many others throughout the camp, for the crematorium explosion. The officer continued strolling around occasionally tapping prisoners for guards to bring up front. Each person appeared healthy compared to everyone else, which struck Teddy as odd.

As the SS officer walked past Teddy, his cologne was a pleasant break from the usual smells around camp. Without looking in his direction, he reached out and tapped Kwart's shoulder. Before Kwart could breathe, he was on his way to the front.

Standing with the group of men facing the line-up, Kwart looked at Teddy, concerned. Not about himself, figuring he would be dead in hours, but for Teddy's well-being. He had watched over Teddy for two years since his family had been deported. He had promised himself that, no matter what happened, he would take care of Teddy. Separated, he could not ensure his safety.

Teddy looked at Kwart, panicked. Kwart was the only constant in his life. Teddy was certain this was the last time they would see each other. No one selected during line-up ever returned. The unspoken farewell was the smell of chimney smoke, yet Teddy longed for his selection. If he went, at least he and Kwart would go together and he was ok with that. Teddy had had enough of Auschwitz-Birkenau. The only good coming out of that place was being able to say goodbye to it.

Teddy dropped his head, defeated. In a few moments, he would be surrounded by thousands of people yet entirely alone. He sighed, coming to terms with what was happening. He had no choice.

Then he felt the tap on his shoulder.

#

17: Chosen Ones

Immediately, Teddy felt a powerful tug on his frail striped prison shirt. His light body moved effortlessly toward the group of men already selected. Teddy counted seven prisoners including himself. Looking back, it was clear the men chosen were in better condition than those left behind.

I wonder why they are choosing healthier men, Teddy thought to himself. *Maybe it was a revolt yesterday and they are killing the strong so it will not happen again?*

The selected prisoners stood in line watching the others march to work detail. An eerie feeling came over Teddy. He was not yet ready to die but yearned for an ending to the life he was living. He found comfort in knowing he would not be alone in the end: Kwart would be with him.

"*Mach Schnell*!" ordered one of the guards.

Without faltering, but not even knowing their final destination, the prisoners marched forward.

They approached one of the gas chambers and crematoria and the smells of burning hair and human flesh became unendurable. Teddy couldn't understand how the *Sonderkommando* – prisoners chosen to dispose of the corpses – dealt with the stench, but then again, what choice did they have.

Each step led the inmates closer to their fate. Teddy questioned if they were going to the gas chambers, like hundreds of thousands of men, women and children before them, or were to be executed while other prisoners observed as a message to those thinking of revolting.

Teddy glanced at the smoking chimneys, seeing birds fly overhead, and shut his eyes briefly. *Why are they free and I am stuck here? What did I do to deserve this?* When he opened his eyes, the chimneys were behind him.

Guards led the group of prisoners past the gas chambers. *OK, so they are going to execute us*, Teddy thought.

They sauntered into the ramp area where Teddy, Kwart and all the other prisoners had arrived at Auschwitz-Birkenau. In front of them were hundreds of other inmates selected for the same fate. Again, Teddy noted that they were stronger than those not chosen.

"Form up!" a soldier yelled, breaking the uneasy silence.

His orders were echoed by other screaming soldiers.

Prisoners began lining up as they did during roll call. Dogs on leashes barked maliciously at frightened Jews, sometimes biting prisoners as they stood in formation. Officers attacked men who were slow to line up, hitting them with gunstocks and kicking them on the ground. Soldiers dragged a few prisoners back into camp.

Everyone around Teddy shook. No one knew what was going on or why they were there. They stood lined up for two hours, unable to make a sound.

A prisoner four people to Teddy's right sneezed. A guard walked up to him and punched him in the face. He grabbed his striped shirt and pulled him out of line. Another guard dragged him back into the camp. Someone else cleared his throat and met the same fate.

Teddy was in a bizarre predicament. He did not know which option was best: standing silent waiting for the unknown or making a sound and going back to camp. He stood there watching everyone, wanting to see what Kwart did first.

A few prisoners coming from the camp with large tins addressed Teddy's questions. The tins were the same used to bring soup during lunchtime. The inmates placed them in front of everyone. It was hard to smell anything over the concentrated fumes coming from the chimneys but Teddy made out the soup.

Why are they feeding us if they are going to kill us? he pondered.

Row by row, the guards allowed men to get their soup and return to the line before eating. When Teddy got back with his soup, he noticed it was thicker than usual. A few more vegetables were in his bowl. He ate it as quickly as his body allowed.

When everyone had finished their soup, the SS officer who'd selected the men addressed the prisoners.

"You pieces of shit have been chosen for your locksmith and metal working skills at another camp. My camp. Do not let me down or I will kill you myself and replace you with someone equally as worthless."

He walked away into a nearby brick building.

The prisoners, relieved they were not going to be killed, relaxed a little. They remained standing for another two hours. Teddy was horrified. He knew nothing about being a locksmith or working with metal. He'd only told the doctor he was a locksmith to save his life.

Teddy passed the time looking around him as he stood in line. To his right were the women's barracks separated from the men by barbed wire. He stared at the women who crowded the fence to see what was happening at the train ramp.

Even with their shaved heads and striped uniforms, Teddy was able to recognize Anna and Rebekah. He tugged Kwart's shirt, motioning with his head for him to look to his right. Kwart's mouth dropped open. He'd assumed the sisters had gone to the gas chambers upon their arrival, but there they stood. He lifted his hand, keeping his arm down by his side, and waved to them. Anna returned the wave, confirming she recognized them as well.

The reunion was short-lived. In the distance, a train was approaching Auschwitz-Birkenau. The men did not know if it was a train with new arrivals or one to take them away.

It slowly pulled through the gate before stopping in front of the prisoners. The train was similar to the one they had ridden on into hell. Teddy was not surprised by the cattle cars.

A sensation of dread came over him. It felt like a lifetime since he'd last experienced the cattle car, but in reality it was only six weeks. The memories flooded back instantly. The smells, stifling heat, no food or water, people dying – the recollections all sent chills down Teddy's spine. He now understood why the Germans had fed them and hoped it would not be long before they ate again.

A few *Sonderkommando* walked to the trains to open the doors. They carried planks to the entrances, which was a rare sight. It was not often Jews walked up planks into trains in Birkenau. They usually exited them that way, heading to their deaths.

As the prisoners entered the cars, *Sonderkommando* handed each of them a small piece of bread. Teddy looked down at the bread and then up at the man and whispered, "Hey, give me a little more." The man handed him another piece. Teddy boarded, promptly walking to the barred window before anyone could get there. He, as well as everyone else, understood the train's torture and knew the window was the best place to stand.

He expected the odor inside the cattle car to be unimaginably dreadful but was surprised to find it smelled of disinfectant.

As the cattle car began filling with men, Teddy prepared himself to be wedged in between people and the wall. Kwart reached around his shoulders, holding on to him so they would be together. Claustrophobia took over. The doors shut. The familiar clunk sounded from the lock outside.

Seeing that no one else was to be loaded, everyone settled down and prisoners began separating. The quarters were tight but the car contained half as many people as during their ride into Auschwitz.

The train shuddered as its rusty wheels squealed to life. Teddy mustered enough energy to pull himself up and look out the window as they pulled out of Auschwitz-Birkenau. Within minutes, the entrance to the camp was behind them, the incessant smoke from the chimneys billowing in the distance.

The chimneys are not the only way out, he thought to himself. Teddy put his hand to his chest feeling his heart beating.

"I am alive," he said aloud without realizing.

Kwart looked down at him and nodded, finding it hard to believe he was too.

The sun set as the train rode westward. Most men remained standing, wide-awake, not knowing when they would arrive at their destination. A few men took off their clogs before sitting or lying down to rest.

Teddy looked out the window occasionally, seeing if he could find signs letting them know where they were headed. When it became too dark to see, Teddy stopped looking.

The train's atmosphere was more relaxed than it had been at Auschwitz-Birkenau. The first few hours of the ride were completely silent. Everyone stayed with their thoughts, processing how they'd managed to leave a place where they were certain they would die.

Sporadically, Teddy inhaled deeply, filling his lungs with fresh air. The uncontaminated sweet scent reminded him he was not dreaming. The men who had taken off their clogs hours earlier moaned in discomfort, and put them back on. The quicklime used to clean the cattle car after each trip had started burning their feet.

No one knew where they were going. They recognized their worries were far from over, but made themselves believe anywhere was better than where they left.

Teddy leaned his head against the thin wooden wall of the cattle car, the vibrations from the track making his teeth rattle. The anxiety and stress of the day caught up with him and he did not have energy left to deal with it for the moment. He shut his eyes, falling asleep where he stood.

The train's wheels let out a loud sustained squeak as it ground to a halt, waking everyone up. Teddy opened his exhausted eyes and looked at the grated window. When the train came to a complete stop, the men inside braced themselves. They stood up, staring at the door and waiting for it to slide open. Their minds flashed back to the last time the doors had opened. For most of them, it was the last time they'd seen their families. The German screams of "*Mach schnell*," and "*Raus schnell*," echoed in their ears. The doors never opened.

A few hours went by but they remained closed. Some men nervously paced back and forth along the walls. The anticipation was becoming too much for them.

The sun had begun to set by the time the train moved again. Teddy's stomach pained with hunger. He had been hopeful, thinking they had stopped for food, but now he was angry that he'd been stupid enough to entertain the thought.

Two days went by. One of the healthier men dropped dead in the center of the car. Teddy and Kwart pulled him to the side but needed the help of a third man. They had become too weak.

Panic was rampant.

"They're going to starve us to death," said one man.

"Then why would they feed us before we boarded?" questioned another.

The train stopped after another two days. The doors opened and guards threw a few loaves of bread into the cattle car. Then the doors slammed shut. Men pounced on the loaves like hungry wolves on prey. Kwart managed to get a decent chunk of bread and he shared it with Teddy.

Teddy knew they were heading west by the direction the sun rose and set each day. He figured they were being taken somewhere in Germany to help the war effort.

As the sun rose on the eighth day, the train squealed to a halt. Dogs barking ferociously told everyone they were at their destination. The men, now much weaker, forced themselves to stand and face the door.

After a few seconds, the clunk of the lock opening rattled the men's knees. The door slid open and a single man walked up into the car.

This is different, Teddy thought.

He expected men to board, yelling and causing chaos, hitting prisoners with gun butts, maybe even another selection, but instead standing in front of him was a single man.

Probably a kapo, Teddy concluded.

The man stood there inspecting everyone. He observed the dead man against the wall and ordered two prisoners to collect him. He moved to the side, clearing a path, and in a sharp tone yelled, "Out!"

The prisoners exited the train and were directed to line up in rows of four. Like at Auschwitz, growling dogs were held back unwillingly around them. Teddy lined up next to Kwart and stood tall. He did not have Sala's shoes for an advantage and was far skinnier than he had been on his arrival at Auschwitz, but there was not going to be a selection.

As prisoners stood in formation, guards handed out camp uniforms and instructed them to change immediately. Established prisoners walked around with bags collecting the old rags from Auschwitz.

Teddy's eyes wandered around the camp, trying to make sense of where they were. He was relieved it did not have any chimneys spewing the smoke of burning bodies. The camp was smaller than Auschwitz-Birkenau. He counted nine wooden barracks. An electrified fence enclosed the perimeter. He also noted four guard towers armed with machine-guns.

The inmates marched into a building and received new haircuts. In Auschwitz-Birkenau, prisoners had shaved Teddy's entire body but in this camp, they just shaved a thick line down the center of his head. Teddy thought the haircut was odd but kept quiet.

The Commandant of the camp called the new arrivals to a roll call and addressed them.

"I am the Commandant. Here you have to work. If you do not do what we say, you will get twenty-five lashings. If I catch one person committing sabotage, because you'll be working with ammunition, I will pick ten people who will be killed with you."

He turned, walking out of sight.

Guards led the men to their new barracks, similar to those in Auschwitz. There were three rows of bunks and thin wooden walls. Teddy was relieved seeing a little bit of straw on the bunks. It was more cushioning than he'd had in months. There were also windows on the walls, which was a luxury. The ability to let fresh air into the barracks was not something they would even dream of in Birkenau.

Teddy wandered up and down the barracks before finding a spot in the middle row of bunks with enough room for both him and Kwart. The conditions remained cramped but left enough room to move around.

The doors swung open, catching everyone's attention. A few prisoners walked in carrying large tins of hot soup. The weary new arrivals lined up. It was the first time they had eaten in four days.

Teddy peeked into a few bowls as men walked by, hoping to see if the soup had more substance, but most of it was already gone by the time they shuffled past.

When it was his turn, he extended his arms taking his bowl of soup. The bowl was heavier than he expected, taking a lot of strength to keep his fingers wrapped around it.

Teddy turned to walk towards his bunk and looked into his bowl. The soup was definitely the thickest he had seen in four years but not by much. It still consisted of mostly water but had a few extra pieces of potato, grouts and rutabaga floating around. He consumed it before reaching his bunk. His stomach craved more although he knew it was impossible. The grumbling had become painful. He reached down to his pant leg, praying for a piece of pork, but it was empty.

Teddy leaned against his bunk staring hopelessly at the empty bowl, trying to will more soup into it. The barracks doors flew open. This time it brought a welcome breeze and an unwelcome figure.

"Line up!" yelled the man.

Frantically, prisoners ran to the bunks and stood upright in front of them.

"You have all been chosen to live a little longer," he said, marching down the center of the barracks. "Most of you are from Lodz and have an ability to work hard and fast," he continued, turning around and pacing. "This camp is Görlitz Biesnitzer Grund."

The man stopped in the center of the barracks, glaring at the prisoners. Sticking his chest out proudly he announced, "I am Jonah Targovetsky, the *Lagerkapo* of this camp. If you decide to slack off or not work to my standards, I will kill you with the same ammunition you will be creating."

He stomped out of the barracks leaving the men thinking about their situation.

The next morning after roll call, the prisoners marched to a munitions factory to work making bombshells and rocket parts.

Teddy had no carpentry or handyman skills and certainly did not know how to work with ammunition, but he learned quickly and worked fast, doing his best to fit in by watching others.

He was surprised when he was placed next to an older woman in the factory. In Auschwitz, the SS had segregated the men from the women. Teddy was blown away when she explained she was not a Jew but rather a resident of the town.

Her name was Helena and she was in her late forties. She'd volunteered to work in the factory to do her part for the war effort. It was the first time in over four years Teddy had communicated with someone living outside whatever barbed wire fence surrounded him.

Helena had lost her son to the Russians on the eastern front a few years earlier and she took an immediate liking to Teddy. His blond hair and blue eyes resembled her son's, as did his fearless personality. She also thought he spoke German beautifully. Teddy looked around the factory, seeing both men and women wearing civilian clothes working adjacent to prisoners.

Through Helena, Teddy was not only able to learn everything he needed to know about munitions but also gathered information about their location and the events happening around them. Helena was his link to the world.

They were located in the German town of Görlitz on the border of Germany and Poland. Half the town spoke Polish or Yiddish and the other half spoke German. Teddy ascertained that Görlitz and the surrounding towns were terrified of the advancing Russians, which was something he in turn shared with the men in his barracks.

Prisoners' eyes grew larger each day as Teddy relayed messages about news from the front.

"They can't get here soon enough," said a prisoner.

"They should've been here years ago," another replied.

The harsh conditions of winter fell upon Görlitz. Overnight, fourteen inches of heavy snow fell on the town. The roof of Teddy's barracks buckled and leaked due to the weight of the snow. Men quivered and screamed as freezing drops trickled on them throughout the night. The lack of space in the bunks could not afford them room to move away from the torturing drips.

The thin wooden exterior walls held no heat and did nothing to stop cold from entering. The men could only rely on body heat to keep them warm. Teddy focused on his memories of Tarzan swinging through the hot jungle but it did nothing to warm him.

At five in the morning, the barracks doors flew open, the biting wind waking up any prisoners who had managed to fall asleep in the first place.

"Everybody up," yelled Jonah Targovetsky, marching heavy-footed and banging a large stick loudly against the wooden bunks. "Get up now," he shouted louder.

Targovetsky was furious. Whatever he was mad about meant trouble for the prisoners. He grabbed prisoners, throwing them to the floor if they moved too slowly to line up, and then kicking them as they rose to their feet.

"Where is he?" Targovetsky screamed.

Teddy looked at everyone, not knowing what was going on or who had pissed Targovetsky off.

"Don't look at him, Teddy, look forward," Kwart reminded him.

Teddy turned his head frontward doing his best to stand at attention, his joints aching from the cold.

"There he is," said a man at the other end of the barracks.

Teddy glanced over to see what was going on. His heart nearly stopped when he noticed where the man was pointing.

He was pointing at Teddy.

#

18: Less than Pigs

"Why was the man pointing at Saba, Dad?" Hayden asked.

"I'll get to that in a second," I answered.

"How are you doing with the story so far, Hayden?" asked Shannon.

"I'm doing ok," she replied. "I don't know if I'd be able to make it through all that if I was there."

"You'd do the best you could," I responded. "I'm sure you'd be ok. You're strong and smart," I continued, reassuring her.

I flicked on the blinker and merged into the left lane of the Tappan Zee Bridge. I looked up into the rearview mirror, grinning at Hayden who smiled in return.

"Only twenty more minutes if everything clears up."

I slammed on the brakes, narrowly missing the Suburban in front of me. My knuckles whitened as I gripped the steering wheel and muttered a few words under my breath.

"Probably longer," Shannon joked.

"Definitely longer," I answered.

#

Targovetsky spun so fast to look at who the man was pointing to that he nearly fell over. He took off sprinting towards Teddy, who had no idea what was going on or why he was the target. Before he had time to figure it out, Targovetsky swung at him with the stick he held, making contact with Teddy's shoulder.

Pain shot through Teddy's entire body as if a truck had hit him. He stayed quiet, hoping whatever was happening would end quicker if he took it and did not complain.

"So you like to tell stories, do you boy?" said Targovetsky.

Teddy looked at him confused. *Stories*? he thought to himself.

"Rumor has it you're telling everyone the Russians are coming," continued Targovetsky.

"They are coming," answered Teddy, before thinking it through.

"And who told you that?" asked Targovetsky.

Teddy remained silent, unwilling to rat out Helena.

"I asked you once and I'll ask one more time. Who told you that?" Targovetsky screamed.

A blow to the stomach answered Teddy's silence. He knelt down to the floor, catching his breath. Kwart reached down to help him back up. His attempt failed. Targovetsky grabbed Kwart's striped prison shirt and looked him in the eyes.

"Don't even think about it," stated Targovetsky. "Everybody line up outside." He glared down at Teddy. "This is going to be one story you remember, boy."

Targovetsky took a few steps back, pointing at Teddy. Two lower level *kapos* walked over and ripped off his clothes. When he was completely nude, the starvation he had endured over four years was clearly visible on his thin body.

The *kapos* dragged him outside into the bitter cold. Snow still fell hard. The prisoners stood trembling in a line-up as the sun began to rise.

"I'll ask you one more time," said Targovetsky. "Who told you the Russians were coming?"

Teddy stared at his fellow inmates. He knew telling Targovetsky Helena informed him about the Russians would not change anything. He would still receive his beating and Helena would suffer the same. He chose silence.

Targovetsky continuously punched Teddy in the face. Blood poured from his nose and mouth, covering the freshly fallen snow with a red sheen. He kicked him in the stomach, dropping him to his knees. The last thing Teddy remembered was the stick in Targovetsky's right hand. Targovetsky wound back and swung. There was a loud crack, then darkness.

Teddy awoke two hours later in the infirmary. His head throbbed with every breath he took and he could barely see through his swollen eyelids.

"I need to cut the lump behind your ear," said the nurse. "I'm not allowed to use anesthesia on you. It's only for Germans."

Teddy nodded, signifying he heard what she said.

"It's going to be painful, so please bear with me," said the nurse. "I'm not allowed to use any medical equipment on you either."

She reached for a dull kitchen knife, placing it in the lit fireplace until the blade glowed yellow. She put it into water, which cooled it down instantly. Teddy could feel the shadow of her hand move over his face to the back of his head, the icy fang touching his skin, then slice. He screamed in agony. The last thing he saw was pus and blood spray across the room before he passed out from the intense pain.

Later, when Teddy awoke, Kwart told him the man who'd called him out had received an extra ration of food for it. It infuriated Teddy to think he could not trust his own people.

A day later, the nurse cleared Teddy to return to work. She secretly told him to stay out of the infirmary because prisoners deemed unworthy to work went to Gross-Rosen concentration camp and were then killed.

Arriving at the factory, Teddy saw Helena standing in her usual spot.

They don't know about her, he thought.

He smiled as he walked to his station. Seeing Teddy, Helena nearly broke down in tears. Kwart had told her what had happened to him and she was grateful that the boy had not exposed her to the authorities.

"Can you go get me some nails, Tanchum?" asked Helena.

"Sure," Teddy responded.

He walked to the corner of the factory where nails were stored. Reaching down to pick up a bucket, Teddy noticed a piece of paper wedged between two wooden floorboards. He pulled at the paper, which shifted one of the boards. Curious, Teddy lifted the plank and was amazed at what he found. Beneath it were a jelly sandwich and an apple Helena had placed there for him. It was her way of saying thank you. From then on, twice a week, Helena asked Teddy to "get her some nails," code for "look under the floorboards".

Despite the risks of having extra food, Teddy shared his sandwich and apple with Kwart and a few other prisoners with whom he had become close.

The sandwich luxury did not last long. Soon the SS forced Teddy to take on a more labor-intensive job because his physical condition was better than that of the other inmates. He was required to roll huge truck tires delivered from trains straight to the factory.

The tires were three times taller than Teddy's tiny, food-deprived frame but he did not care. Rolling tires made him feel like a kid again. He pretended he was in Lodz, hitting his bicycle tire down Mielczarskiego Street with the aluminum tube he'd fashioned.

Most people taller than Teddy were only able to roll one tire at a time and struggled. Teddy pushed two tires at once and made it look easy. He caught the attention of an SS Officer walking by.

"You work well," said the officer.

"Thank you, I'm trying," answered Teddy in German.

The SS officer reached down into his coat pocket from which he pulled out a piece of bread and handed it to Teddy. He petted Teddy's head like a pet dog and walked away. Teddy was shocked. He could not understand why the German had given him a piece of bread. It did not make sense to him. *One second he's handing out bread and the next he's killing someone*. Teddy decided it was best not to mull it over. He ate the bread and kept working.

Each day, as prisoners marched between the factory and their barracks, they watched the camp commandant walk into a small barracks carrying two buckets loaded to the brim with food for his prized pigs. Frequently, apple cores, potato peelings and other rotten pieces of food fell out of the buckets into the snow. Prisoners broke formation, running after the food, but were always beaten for leaving the line. They did not mind as long as they had got something extra to eat.

One day, agonizing hunger and bitter cold got the better of Teddy. He decided he was going to attempt the impossible and raid the pigsty. Kwart tried reasoning with him but Teddy would not have it.

"You'll be killed for sure, Tanchum," said Kwart.

"I'll be fine," Teddy promised. "And we'll all benefit from it."

Teddy waited until after roll call before sneaking away. With everyone face deep in their tin bowls of supper, he tiptoed out of the door, heading for the pigs' barracks. Thick snow on the ground made it difficult to manoeuver and expended most of Teddy's energy.

Once there, he searched for a way to enter unseen. He knew that the front door – in plain view of everyone – was not an option. The barracks had no side windows either. Suddenly, out of the silence, Esther's laugh grabbed his attention. He trudged around the building's perimeter in the direction of the laugh, finally finding a small window on the back wall. Teddy looked around the area but there was no sign of a girl having been there.

He jumped, grabbed the ledge and started pulling himself up. His emaciated body had no trouble climbing through the metal bars in front of the window. As his feet touched the dirt floor, he was surprised to feel it was soft and warm.

These damn pigs have a heated barracks! he thought.

Teddy walked past a few caged rabbits and over to the pigs who were too busy gorging themselves to notice him petting their heads. He peeked into their trough and took a deep breath as he admired its beauty. Even though most of the food was spoiled or half eaten, it was the largest bounty Teddy had seen for as long as he remembered.

He reached down and began loading his pockets, stopping to consume a half-eaten corncob and a few potato peelings before continuing. He tucked his shirt into his pants and loaded potato skins, carrots and a few chunks of beef into it, making sure not to stuff it too much to bring attention to himself. He headed back towards the window.

Teddy stepped on an empty crate to lift himself up to the window ledge. As he opened it and started sliding through, he panicked, realizing he could not fit. The food made him too large.

He dropped down to the floor, then sat on the crate, contemplating what to do. He could not return to his barracks empty-handed or he would never hear the end of it. After thinking for a minute, Teddy stood up and walked over to the trough. He grabbed a corncob then snuck to the front entrance. He opened the door a crack, peeking outside.

To his amazement, the grounds in front of him were completely devoid of guards. Seizing his opportunity, Teddy strolled out of the pigs' barracks towards his own, peering back to see if anyone noticed.

As he turned his head, two other prisoners entered the pigsty through the front door. They must have admired Teddy's courage and the prize that came with having it. Teddy, recognizing he still held the corncob in his hand, jammed it into his pocket. He looked back up in time to see his nightmare become reality.

The two men were leaving the barracks through the front door, as Teddy had done, but they were spotted. Targovetsky approached them, screaming. He punched one of the prisoners in the face before having them escorted away.

Kwart was relieved to see Teddy enter the barracks unscathed. He kissed both of his cheeks, and gave him a hug. Teddy pulled his shirt away from his body allowing Kwart to get a view of the bounty while telling him the story of the two men who were caught.

"I'm thankful for what you have, Tanchum, but you're never to attempt this again, you understand?" said Kwart.

Teddy nodded, hearing sincerity in Kwart's voice. The two of them secretly ate the stash of food, then got rid of any evidence in case the guards decided to search the barracks.

That night, SS guards stripped the two captured prisoners naked and tied their hands behind them. They were marched to the center of the square, where they were hung from a tree by their bound hands. The awkward position caused incredible pain in their shoulders. To make matters worse, the guards placed buckets of water with tiny holes above their heads, allowing icy water to drip continuously on them.

Their screams echoed throughout the camp. Teddy did not sleep. He could not comprehend how he had made it through the front door unnoticed while only moments later the SS had caught the other two inmates.

The next morning, the commandant ordered roll call for the entire camp. *Kapos* lined prisoners facing inwards toward an open area. Guards cut the two men down from the tree and dragged them to the center of the square.

The camp Commandant and Targovetsky stood in the center waiting for the prisoners. When they arrived, one of the prisoners ran to the Commandant, dropping down to his knees. He begged for his life and forgiveness, kissing his boots. The other prisoner stood facing forward at attention, motionless.

The Commandant kicked the begging Jew off his feet and walked up to the prisoner standing at attention. He reached down decidedly, pulled out his pistol and shot the man in the chest. The prisoner's body dropped to the ground, rolling and flopping like a fish out of water before eventually coming to a stop. The Commandant told the other man to line up.

He then addressed the prisoners.

"You are going to march to Tirol. Those of you who do not want to go or are too weak, step to the right side of the square."

Three hundred debilitated men made their way to the right, a few of them helping others walk across the snow-covered field.

After the prisoners separated, the Commandant asked those willing to walk if they had good wooden shoes. If they did not, he told them to come to the center of the square.

Teddy's left shoe had a splinter on the sole that felt like it pierced his skin with each step he took. He decided to step forward into the center. The last thing he wanted was to go for a long march dealing with the pain.

Hermann Tschech was a German and a prisoner in the camp. Before the war, he'd been a murderer and had served many years in prison for his crimes, but in Görlitz, he'd become the camp elder.

Considered the big man in charge of prisoners, he used his persuasive skills to influence the Commandant and other German authorities.

Hermann came over to stand next to the Commandant. He stepped in front of the men with bad shoes and instructed them to take good shoes from the prisoners too weak to march.

The inmates headed over to the right side of the square, taking shoes from the weaker prisoners. Teddy walked to a man who was holding his shoes out readily, and said thank you while taking them. The icy snow made the man's legs shake and he could barely stand. As Teddy bent down to put on the shoes, the man leaned over to rest on him. Targovetsky walked over and gave him a jab in his kidney, yelling at him to stand up. Slowly the man lifted himself, trying his best to remain upright.

Hermann called out to the men receiving new shoes to line up. He selected fifteen of them to help gather large wagons from the city to carry supplies and food. Teddy was chosen. The Commandant ordered the prisoners too weak to go on the march to enter inside Block 2 and await further instructions.

The fifteen men loaded the wagons with supplies and food rations. While pulling a wagon towards camp, Teddy overheard Hermann speaking to a few prisoners. He bragged about persuading the Commandant to allow the march to Tirol. He'd heard from a few people temporarily staying in town that the Russians planned to bypass Görlitz, not seeing it as an obstacle. He heard from the same people that the Russians were heading to Tirol, and had managed to negotiate some sort of deal with the Commandant to permit the march. He never mentioned what the agreement was.

Teddy and the fourteen men pulling the large, heavy wagons stopped in front of Block 2. The Commandant and Hermann whispered to each other while SS guards closed in. Hermann opened the door, screaming at everyone to step outside.

The three hundred weak and unwilling prisoners ran barefoot into the snow, lining up. The Commandant ordered them to pull the loaded wagons for the duration of the march as their punishment for being weak.

#

19: Walking Dead

It was mid-February and the temperature dropped down to zero degrees Fahrenheit as the march began. Three hundred sick men and women stayed in Görlitz to clean camp. What appeared to be a thousand men and half as many women formed two straight lines on either side of the road walking towards Tirol. The prisoners, wearing ragged, striped prison garb, did not stand a chance against the biting cold. Even SS officers wearing their heavy winter coats and snow boots could not control their shaking.

The miserable conditions worsened as snow began to fall, making simple tasks nearly impossible to complete. Teddy walked behind Kwart who felt the full wrath of the subzero temperature. Occasionally, Teddy reached out to rub Kwart's back, hoping the friction caused some heat, but it only stung his painfully numb hands. Some Germans glared at the marching prisoners, heartlessly smiling at them as if they were herding animals.

Five kilometers into the march, the prisoners arrived at the village of Kunsserdorf. They piled into a few horse stables reeking of fresh manure but at least they were out of the cold. A few prisoners placed their hands over the steaming manure, pulling some warmth from it. Others sat down, glad to be off their feet.

An announcement circulated through the stables that Hermann had gone back to Görlitz to collect a few more sick prisoners for the march. That was followed by another announcement that the wagon carrying the bread had been stolen, dropping the extremely meager rations down to almost nothing.

"I bet Hermann and his followers are eating our bread right now," said a prisoner.

"Don't say that out loud or you'll be the next person he murders," answered another.

Teddy leaned on Kwart as the two sat on a bale of hay, staring into the stable.

"Do you really think they're taking us to Tirol?" asked Teddy.

"I don't know what to believe," answered Kwart.

A few hours later Hermann arrived with one hundred and fifty additional prisoners. Everyone lined back up and continued marching. The sun was setting, bringing the temperature down with it. Every muscle and bone in Teddy's body ached as he marched through the unforgiving cold. Twelve people had died in the hours spent at Kunsserdorf. There was no time to bury them so prisoners lined them up on the floor in one of the stables, leaving them for whoever came next.

Teddy's stomach cramped up on him. He had not eaten since the morning but pressed on, not wanting to show weakness to the Germans. Another man succumbed to cramping, bending over to grab his stomach. Before he had time to regain his composure and continue marching, a soldier shot him. The line of men and women did their best not to step on him as they walked by, not wanting to slow the pace.

More and more dead bodies lined the road as the march persisted. Some had visible bullet wounds while others had starved or frozen to death. It did not matter which way they perished, they all lay where they fell and stayed there until someone else found them.

About halfway to the village of Friedersdorf, the march halted and the Jews stood still in the freezing cold. A German soldier picked a few of them to grab wagons and follow him. The men disappeared for a while and everyone waiting assumed they were dead.

After two hours, all of the men returned pulling wagons filled with sugar beets. It had been days since they last ate anything. The sugar beets ripped into the prisoners' throats, but they did not care as long as they were eating.

As they continued marching, the terrain became impassable. They faced sheer inclines up sides of mountains and down steeper declines. Teddy held on to Kwart, slowly making their way forward.

"How far have we gone, Kwart?" Teddy asked.

"I don't know, just keep moving," said Kwart, raising his voice just high enough for Teddy to hear over the wind but low enough to be undetected by the Germans.

The snow made the poorly surfaced roads extremely slippery and wooden shoes created no friction. One man fell and broke his leg. Unable to move forward on his own, he was shot on the spot.

As they approached the village of Sohland, Teddy's heart jumped, feeling the rush of adrenaline. It was going to be a night he would sleep indoors.

The men were confined to two small stables while the women slept in one large barn. In order to make more room to sleep, some of the men climbed up to the attic where large wooden planks spanned the width of the stables. They placed straw over the beams, soon falling fast asleep.

In the distance, the prisoners heard bombardments and explosions. Rumors spread around the stables that the Russians were close. The men spoke of liberation.

Teddy lay on the ground staring up at the roof of the barn. The frigid wind howled outside making the rickety structure creak. He thought about his family. Anka went through his mind. He figured it was best he'd left the doll in Lodz. It would have certainly been taken away at Auschwitz and probably cost him his life.

He thought about the children screaming that first night in Birkenau and how he was glad he'd been by himself long before that night, especially after hearing what would have happened to his family if they'd made it to Auschwitz.

Teddy reflected on himself that night. He'd lost his childhood and hated the Germans for forcing him to grow up quickly. He questioned if the things he was doing would make his family proud.

Two men crashed down from the beams above. One let out a painful scream as he landed on the hard dirt floor. The other did not say anything. He'd broken his neck and died instantly. The injured prisoner crawled over to an open area on the floor and went into the fetal position. A few inmates checked on him. He moaned endlessly as they poked and prodded his body. It was determined that he'd broken a few ribs which were easily seen through his skin-and-bones body. The next morning he was dead. One of the ribs had punctured his left lung. It had filled up with blood and the man had suffocated. Without hesitation, a few prisoners searched his pockets for food or anything useful, but they were empty. Disappointed, they walked away, leaving him there until roll call.

For the next few days, the prisoners remained in Sohland. They constantly scrounged for food. Teddy, like everyone else, raided the village garbage hoping to find anything edible. He occasionally found scraps but nothing coming close to ending his hunger.

Sugar beets seemed to be the only rations around town. The beets wreaked havoc on the prisoners' throats but were tolerated because they were edible.

Dysentery spread around the prisoners, killing a few of them. Their frail, starving, immune-deficient bodies did not stand a chance against it.

When there was nothing left to eat in the village, it was time to move on. The extreme food deprivation made prisoners question whether they had enough energy to keep moving. Hermann Tschech promised everyone, as he had the entire time, there would be food for them in Tirol.

Ukrainian soldiers stepped up in place of the SS officers who headed back to Görlitz to take care of business. The Ukrainians were worse than the SS in many regards. They viewed the Jews as dogs and treated them accordingly. The death rate increased drastically after they took over.

They took roll call before the march continued. Quite a few prisoners had died during the stay in Sohland. Accidents, hunger and the freezing cold all captured the lives of their victims.

"Who here is unable to go on?" Herman Tschech asked, shouting forcefully over the wind. "Step forward to the front if you can no longer march."

Nine men moved up to the front of roll call. Hermann told them to stand to the side. Everyone able to march received an extremely small portion of rutabaga and sugar beets while those who could not march watched them eat.

Teddy and three other men selected to stay behind got an extra rutabaga. Tschech charged the group with cleaning up the stables and barns where everyone had stayed. Too cold to go outside, most of the men who'd slept in the stables had relieved their bowels in one corner of the building.

As they cleaned the stables, the nine men who were not going to continue with the march remained lined up out in the freezing cold.

One of the cleaners shoveling the pile of human excrement ended up falling face first into the feces when his wooden shovel handle snapped. Muttering a few words under his breath, he continued to work.

When Teddy and the men had finished cleaning, they reported outside to the Ukrainians. There were two wagons parked in front of the large barn. A Ukrainian soldier yelled at the nine men, telling them to get onto one of the wagons. As they sat down, another Ukrainian told Teddy and the three other cleaners to load the dead bodies onto the wagon as well.

After loading four dead bodies, the wagon took off with the nine men. A Ukrainian ordered Teddy to load the other wagon with shovels and pick axes. He immediately knew what it meant but tried to convince himself it was not happening.

Three Ukrainians stepped up onto the wagon. One of them told the driver to get moving and they took off. Teddy and the three other men walked alongside. It was a pitch-black night. Thick clouds covered the moon and stars, allowing no light to pass through. The clip clop of horse hooves and sound of the rolling wheels were the only things letting Teddy know he was going in the right direction.

Teddy knew a few of the men in the first wagon. Three of them were from Lodz. One had lived a street over from his apartment on Mielczarskiego Street, and another had a daughter who'd played with Esther on occasion. The two once fought over Anka, resulting in a tear under her elbow.

The driver pulled back on the reins, causing the horse to neigh. The wagon slowed to a stop near the edge of a forest. The first wagon was there waiting.

Two Ukrainians threw shovels and pick axes at Teddy and the other prisoners who'd walked to the forest and told them to start digging. Following orders, Teddy picked up a shovel and went to work.

Watching what was happening, the nine men on the wagon began weeping hysterically. Each one of them begged to be allowed to return to the march, explaining they were more than capable. One of the men begged a soldier, "I do not want to die." The Ukrainian spat on him.

A boy only a year older than Teddy ran from soldier to soldier, pleading with them to let him live. No one paid him any attention. As Teddy continued digging, tears escaped his eyes. He knew the inevitable was going to happen, regardless of the petitioning, and he was completely helpless to do anything but watch.

With the ditch completed, the nine men knelt down facing their final resting place. A single Ukrainian went down the line shooting them all in the head, one by one, their bodies falling into the grave.

The Ukrainian executioner ordered Teddy and the three other prisoners to cover up the ditch before rejoining the group.

All along the way, corpses of those who had fallen during the march lined the road. It was easy to tell those who had been murdered and those succumbing to the cold and hunger by the blood staining the snow around them, or the lack of.

Occasionally they would walk over people still alive. Teddy wanted badly to bend down and help them, but knew the penalty if he tried. He put his head down and carried on.

The men picked up their pace. Finally, they caught up to the march as the sun began rising. Their bodies were exhausted from the lack of food and over-exertion of energy. Teddy snuck up behind Kwart to tap him on the shoulder. Turning to see Teddy, Kwart smiled, giving him a hug and a kiss on both cheeks.

"I didn't know if I'd see you again," said Kwart.

They spent one day and night in Lehdehauser. As everyone readied to continue marching after roll call, a few men convinced Teddy and Kwart to escape with them. They planned to hide in a few bales of hay. When the others left and were out of sight, they would sneak out the other way.

As the march began, the inmates planning to escape hid in piles of hay in a barn. A bad feeling came over Teddy. He turned to Kwart, saying he wanted to continue with the rest of the prisoners. Kwart agreed. As they rejoined the march, a few Ukrainians broke off and headed into the barn. Gunshots blared as they fired entire clips into the bales of hay killing most of the men hiding there.

Later that day, they entered the town of Rennersdorf. A few hours into their stay, townsfolk informed them that Russians were everywhere and all roads were closed so they would have to stay in Rennersdorf until further notice.

The men stayed in horse stables with large stalls filled with manure. With no other place to sleep, they laid down on the droppings. In the morning, worms covered their bodies and they relied on each other to remove them all.

After two weeks of sleeping in the dung, everyone had had enough and moved to tight quarters next to each other on the floor. Most people had diarrhea and needed to get up several times throughout the night. They stepped on everyone as they tried to get to the bathroom. On occasion, they slipped and lost their balance, losing control of their bowels over prisoners underneath them.

As each day went by, talk of liberation increased. Everyone envisioned the Russians appearing any minute. Cannons fired in the distance. Although they never seemed to be getting any closer, the fact they were there boosted everyone's morale.

After three weeks in Rennersdorf, the Ukrainians concluded they would not be able to make it to Tirol. The Russians were blocking their path. They decided the prisoners could not stay in Rennersdorf any longer and needed to return to Görlitz.

Hermann Tschech addressed the prisoners at roll call, again asking anyone too weak to march to step forward. He informed them trucks would take them back to Görlitz.

Knowing the fate of the nine men too weak to march last time, Teddy decided to walk. However, over one hundred and fifty men stepped forward. They were all loaded onto trucks and driven away.

The march back to Görlitz took two days. The weather was warmer and the roads clear. Intermittently, Teddy heard shots fired behind him. Each one was the end of somebody needing to slow down his pace.

Arriving in Görlitz, Teddy was surprised to see the men who had been driven off in trucks waiting for them. The Commandant ordered the prisoners to line up. A few trucks with hundreds of shovels and pick axes pulled up.

"Start digging," said the Commandant.

#

20: Homecoming

The munitions factory had been shut down for a few weeks already by the time the march re-entered camp. The Russians had captured the town where the factory received its raw materials and no shipments were coming in. Instead, the prisoners needed to dig anti-tank ditches in the middle of city streets.

On the second day in camp, Teddy's barracks lined up in their usual roll call. Teddy had not slept the previous night. He was burning up with a high fever and had terrible diarrhea. He raised his hand to tell the *kapo* he could not work.

Targovetsky walked up to Teddy, leaning in close to his face.

"So you don't feel well enough to work?" he questioned.

"No sir, I'm burning up," answered Teddy.

Targovetsky grabbed him by his striped shirt. He yanked him forward, placing him in front of everyone.

"I have an announcement to make," said Targovetsky, sarcastically. "Little Teddy Z doesn't feel well today. I'm going to make him feel better."

He pulled out a leather strap. Another *kapo* came up with a wooden stool and bent Teddy over it, holding tightly onto his outstretched arms.

The first lash sent searing pain through Teddy's body. His shriek made the other prisoners cringe. They wanted to say something to Targovetsky but knew it would only result in a flogging of their own.

Teddy did not have time to recover from the first lash when the second ripped into his skin. He bawled uncontrollably. His body, now a mere skeleton, could not handle the whipping.

Teddy passed out after the third lashing. It was not until a few hours later when he awoke in his barracks that Kwart told him he'd received twenty-five lashes. His body had swollen, making it hard to move, and his skin was red and hot to the touch.

Kwart helped Teddy to the infirmary. At first, he fought Kwart about going because of the warning the nurse had given him when he was last there. He wanted no part of being sent to Gross-Rosen.

Teddy had a high fever. His joints ached as badly as the lashes seared his skin.

A few minutes later Targovetsky entered the infirmary to check on him. He walked over to the table, leaning Teddy forward to look at the marks left by the lashes he'd given him.

"Now there is a reason not to work today," said Targovetsky, patting Teddy on his back.

Teddy winced but did not dare make eye contact with him. Targovetsky turned around and walked out.

A week later, Teddy was back digging anti-tank ditches with the rest of the prisoners. He worked with a shovel while another prisoner his age used a pick axe.

On the right side of the road located next to the ditch Teddy was digging was a butcher's shop. There, hanging on hooks in the window of the shop, were long sleeves of salami. The sight of the long rolls of cured meat drove Teddy crazy. It became hard for him to concentrate as he constantly caught himself staring into the shop window.

The saliva in Teddy's mouth built up so much he began to drool. He looked around taking in his situation.

His odds were better than usual because the SS no longer watched over them. Most of them had left Görlitz in a panic as the Russians closed in. German soldiers of the Wehrmacht had replaced them. They were young and as hopeful as the prisoners that the war would end soon.

Teddy looked back at the shop and saw the butcher standing outside the front door. Making eye contact with him, Teddy pointed to his mouth, hoping the butcher would understand what he was asking for.

In response, the butcher pointed his chin in the direction of the soldiers standing on the other side of the road. Teddy gazed over his shoulder at the guards, waiting for his moment.

Leaning in to the boy working next to him, Teddy whispered, "Hey, I am going to try to get salami."

"They'll kill you if they catch you," answered a voice behind Teddy.

Alarmed, Teddy turned around to see a young soldier standing behind him. The boy had to be the same age as Teddy. His jacket appeared two sizes too big and his helmet did not fit properly. Remaining calm and assessing the situation Teddy repeated what the soldier said in his head.

"*THEY'LL kill you if THEY catch you.*"

The soldier had separated himself from the rest of the group. Teddy's mind went into bargaining mode.

"I'll split it with you if I get it," offered Teddy.

The young soldier did not say anything in return. He walked away.

Teddy looked over at the soldiers on the other side of the street but they had gone. Seizing his opportunity, he took off running into the butcher's shop, unseen. Once inside, Teddy looked around the store. There was a large variety of meats hanging. The smell drove him crazy. His stomach could not contain itself and growled with anticipation.

The butcher was a big husky man with a graying beard and mustache. He hurried out from behind the counter past Teddy to the front door. He locked it and pulled down the shade in front of the window.

"Wait a minute," said the butcher, in a low burly voice.

He walked to the back of the store, out of sight. Teddy quietly snuck behind the counter, stealing three long pieces of salami which he stuffed into the sleeves of his striped shirt. He nipped back around the counter, returning to where he had stood seconds earlier.

Minutes felt like hours as time went by. Teddy did not know what was going on. He could not leave the store because the butcher had locked the door. He began panicking. *What if he went to get the Germans, or worse, the Ukrainians?* Teddy thought.

Footsteps approached. Teddy relaxed on seeing the butcher come back into sight by himself. He carried a large brown bag, making Teddy's eyes grow wide. The butcher handed it to Teddy who quickly opened it to look inside. It was packed with salamis and bread.

Teddy looked up at the butcher with the widest smile he had given in over five years. The butcher nodded at Teddy, understanding his appreciation. Reaching down, he placed his hand on Teddy's shoulder.

"Make sure they don't catch you with this, you understand?"

He unlocked the door and returned behind the counter. It took Teddy five minutes to find his opportunity to run back to his ditch. When he made it, his fellow worker could not believe his eyes on seeing the brown bag.

A minute later, Teddy saw the young soldier walking around. He motioned to him to come over to the ditch. For keeping quiet, Teddy gave him an entire salami. The soldier thanked him and walked away. Teddy and his fellow digger were shell-shocked. It was the first time a German had ever been polite to them.

That night in the barracks, the prisoners had the biggest celebration they'd experienced in years, although it was mixed with fear of punishment. Teddy shared his salami and bread with everyone. Men broke down into tears as they ate the meat. The taste was indescribable. The flavors exploded in their mouths. Most of them could not remember what real food tasted like.

The next morning, the entire barracks was sick with diarrhea. Not used to such indulgences their bodies had rejected the rich food, but no one minded. The celebration was something they would never forget.

Once the prisoners had completed the anti-tank ditches inside the city, they moved outside of its walls. People urged Teddy to escape daily. Outside of the city, there was nothing to stop him. He was blond-haired, blue-eyed and spoke perfect German which meant he would blend in easily with the general population.

The truth was that Teddy did not know where to go if he escaped. He would not have anywhere to sleep or anything to eat. He felt safer with the other prisoners than off on his own and could not bear the thought of leaving Kwart.

In a matter of days, the prisoners were digging along the front lines of the war. There were dogfights in the air daily and loud cannon fire rang in their ears. The anticipation of the Russians' arrival boosted prisoners' morale to levels not felt since before the war. Men ran around barracks whispering, "Any day now." The fact their job was to dig ditches preventing the arrival of their rescuers ate at the prisoners constantly. Every shovel of dirt accompanied an equal weight in curses for the SS.

On May 7, 1945, the Commandant spoke to the prisoners while they stood at attention for morning roll call.

"According to my commanding officers, I have an order to set you free. You can go anywhere you want and do anything you would like, but I suggest you stay in camp. There will be many bombardments in the following days. Good luck with your lives."

He took a few steps back before turning and walking off.

Teddy could not believe his ears. He was free. The liberated prisoners let out cheers and hugged everyone around them. A few men dropped to their knees, gazing up at the sky, their cheeks glistening from the sun shining on their tears.

The men scattered around the square, no longer needing to stand in roll call formation. Some immediately ran out of the perimeter and into the streets of Görlitz. Others wandered freely around the camp. It was the first time in many years the men were able to do what they pleased.

Teddy and Kwart followed a few former prisoners to the SS cafeteria barracks. They walked inside to search the area for food. They felt awkward scrounging around the empty barracks, as if they were not supposed to be there. Moments earlier guards would have shot them if they'd entered the building, now no one cared. Fresh in Teddy's mind were visions of the SS eating with the plates and silverware he now scavenged. He could almost hear the clicking and clanking of fork on dish as if they were still there.

Teddy heard German voices around behind the barracks. He cautiously walked towards them. There, he saw the Commandant addressing a few SS officers. Reaching out, he shook each one by the hand. One by one, the men walked out of sight.

Kwart walked up behind Teddy and peeked around the corner to see what he was looking at. The Commandant leaned down, giving his German Shepherd a hug and a kiss on its nose. He stood up and wiped his eyes, pulled out his pistol and shot the dog. He stepped into his car and the driver drove out of the camp.

Kwart ran inside the SS barracks, returning two minutes later with a knife. He approached the dog. Teddy stepped out from around the building and followed him. As they neared the fatally wounded dog, it shook in agony on the ground. Kwart reached down, petting it gently for a few seconds. He grabbed the dog's snout and lifted it towards him while cutting its throat with the knife. A few seconds later the dog stopped shaking.

Kwart carried the dog into the kitchen and began skinning it. Teddy searched the cabinets for other food to eat. He found a few potatoes, carrots and an onion. He grabbed a pot which he filled with water, then threw in the vegetables and began making a soup. Once the dog was skinned, cleaned and quartered, Kwart dropped it into the pot of boiling water with the vegetables.

The soup was the greatest thing Teddy ever tasted. He could not remember the last time he'd eaten fresh meat or a soup as thick as he wanted. It was their first meal as free men.

Nobody slept that night. The bombardments sounded like they were directly overhead. Teddy's mind flashed back to five years earlier when he'd huddled with his family on the bedroom floor as the Germans approached Lodz.

Each time a shell hit the ground, the earth shook. The men crowded the bottom bunks, afraid the barracks would collapse. One brave soul was crazy enough to climb on top of the factory chimney and hang a white flag. Men prayed aloud for the shells to miss the camp.

"We didn't live to die like this," screamed one man, loud enough for the entire barracks to hear.

There was an unnatural silence in Görlitz as the sun rose. The air was thick with the scents of expended cannon and mortar shells and an eerie fog hovered over the ground.

The squealing of tank wheels on tracks broke the stillness. The men crawled out of their bunks to see the commotion first-hand. Exhausted from a sleepless night, Teddy and Kwart joined the rest of the prisoners exiting the barracks.

Everyone convened in the square where three Russian tanks and a jeep were parked.

A few Russian soldiers got out of their tanks and stared in horror at the sight of the walking skeletons approaching them. Prison uniforms hung from their skin-and-bones bodies. Most hobbled towards the soldiers in an unnatural, painful gait, needing assistance to press forward.

A man stepped out of the jeep, gazing at the former prisoners. Teddy could tell by his pressed uniform and clean face he was the officer in charge of the Russians around Görlitz.

The Russian officer addressed the group.

"You have three days. We do not see. We do not hear. Do whatever you like."

#

21: Finding Oneself

The men cheered at the words of the Russian officer. Most of them ran out of the camp taking full advantage of their newfound freedom.

At first, the newly-freed prisoners' main concern was taking care of the SS around Görlitz. They searched buildings and alleyways in the city, but the more they looked, the more discouraged they became. The SS had disappeared, fleeing at the first sight of the Russian army. A couple of men laughed at the thought of what they would actually do to an SS soldier if they found one. They were skeletons, barely having enough strength to walk down the road let alone beat a trained soldier to death.

A few healthier Jews captured soldiers of the Wehrmacht who'd been guilty of treating them poorly and got their revenge. It was a strange sight for Teddy. Suddenly, the tide had shifted and those devoid of power became powerful. It also scared Teddy, who turned away, cringing at the sight of things happening around him. The way some of his fellows acted made him think of the SS themselves. He promised himself never to do something he could envision the SS doing.

Walking the streets of Görlitz with Kwart, Teddy witnessed the looting of many shops by former prisoners. Windows were broken as people made their own entrances into stores to steal whatever they wanted. His mind fell back to the kindness of the butcher who had given him salamis and bread for the barracks.

Teddy changed direction, quickly making his way to the butcher's shop. He somehow needed to find a way to ensure the store remained safe.

He and Kwart picked up their pace and bumped into a few Russian soldiers smoking cigarettes on a street corner. In Russian, Teddy asked the soldiers to go with him. Interested in the little boy's enthusiasm, the Russians flicked their smokes away before following him to the shop.

The butcher stood in front of his shop wielding a broom, ready to defend it against anyone coming to steal his meat. Watching the group of soldiers approach him with Teddy in the lead, the butcher did not know what to think. He lowered his broom as the group neared.

In fluent Russian, Teddy explained to the soldiers that the butcher was a good man and had risked his own life when he had given him and his barracks bread and salami. He asked if there was anything they could do to protect his shop.

One soldier left the pack to speak with someone. In the meantime, the butcher went into his shop and returned with a few pieces of cured meat, which he handed to the small crowd in front of the store.

Twenty minutes later the soldier returned with the high-ranking officer who had addressed the Jews when they arrived. Teddy repeated the story to him.

"This man saved my life and the lives of the men in my barracks," explained Teddy.

Impressed by the butcher's bravery and willingness to help despite dire consequences, the officer offered to contract out the butcher to supply his troops with meat for the duration of their occupation in Görlitz.

The butcher wept, knowing his shop would be safe from looters. He hugged Teddy, and gave him salami to share with Kwart as a way to thank him. Then they parted ways.

Teddy and Kwart went into apartments, like the rest of the freed prisoners, looting what they could find. Many residences were vacant. Their owners had fled before the bombardments began, uncertain if their buildings would be damaged or if the propaganda about the barbaric actions of invading Russians was true.

The apartments themselves had jewelry and a few other things of value, but basements held the largest bounties. Boxes of marmalade, meats and canned vegetables were stacked from floor to ceiling. Teddy crammed as much food into his tiny stomach as it could handle, often getting sick from overeating.

Teddy and Kwart spent a month in Görlitz after liberation. After that, they decided they'd had enough of looting diamonds and money and wanted to go back to Lodz to try to start their lives over again.

One night, they crept into a farm on the outskirts of the city. Creeping over to the chicken coop, Teddy lifted a few of the sleeping birds to take some eggs.

Kwart walked over to the stable to take a horse while Teddy made his way to a small barn a hundred yards away to commandeer a wagon. Out of the corner of his eye, he saw a red bicycle leaning on the side of the barn. He ran over, grabbed it, and placed it in the wagon to take back to Lodz.

After strapping the horse to the wagon unnoticed, Teddy and Kwart started making their way home. The world was too busy dealing with problems on the borders of war-torn countries to worry about dirt roads heading inland. They travelled as far as they could during the day and stopped close to farms at night. Teddy ran through the fields picking fresh vegetables while Kwart went into the chicken coops stealing eggs and a few chickens for meat. They would get up before farmers began tending their fields and continue travelling.

On the road, Teddy spent his time reflecting. Not only on the things that had happened over the previous five years but also on how much he'd changed in that time. He was ten when he entered into the ghetto. The Nazis traded his innocence as a child, playing on the streets and in fields, for a life of stealing and hard labor. Teddy could not understand how he'd survived and thought it best not to dwell on it too much. He chose to not let hate overwhelm him and instead used it to inspire him. He thought a lot about his family. Were they dead? Had they gone to a work camp? Could they have survived? Were they together?

Teddy was going back to Lodz as a sixteen-year-old man. He had seen and lived through unimaginable things that no one should experience in countless lifetimes, and yet he could barely remember how to read or write. His education had stopped while he was in elementary school. There had been no use for it in his life.

The arrival in Lodz was bittersweet. The familiar smells of home flooded Teddy's nose as they rode the wagon into the city. They looked all around them, taking in the view, while pinching their cheeks to make sure they were not dreaming. The reality of where they were began to sink in. Flower boxes hanging from windows brought back visions of Teddy planting million bells with Touba every year around his birthday at the end of May. The lettering of the streets signs reminded him of Simcha, the *Kuncenmaller* of Lodz.

Nothing has changed, Teddy thought. The city had remained undamaged throughout the war and not been targeted during bombing raids. The recognizable sound of horse hooves pounding cobblestone streets brought Teddy back to the fateful wagon ride he took with his mother and younger sister to the hospital's deportation holding area. He shook off the thought, looking up from the stone road to see a permanent scar on the preserved city's face. Not everything had remained the same. In front of the wagon was a vacant lot. The plot of land, which once held the beautiful Stara Synagogue, was empty. The memories of his grandfather, its cantor, and his father's stained glass windows had been taken with it.

One by one, vacant lots appeared. The temples previously standing there had failed to remain.

"Maybe they'll be rebuilt," said Teddy, wishing everything would return to how he remembered.

"Maybe," answered Kwart.

Overall, the city appeared visually intact, but mentally and emotionally, it was completely different. It felt cold. Teddy and Kwart walked along city streets they had been banned from years earlier. They did not know anyone in the city anymore, and nor did they know what had happened to the people they used to know. Polish people, who had not lifted a finger to help them when they needed it and supported the Nazi cause, surrounded them. Once again, they found themselves amongst people yet entirely alone.

Teddy and Kwart separated temporarily to figure things out for themselves. Kwart went searching for Anna and Rebekah. Seeing them as he'd boarded the train out of Birkenau gave him a tiny sliver of hope they were alive. Teddy headed back to his childhood apartment.

He rounded the corner, heading up Mielczarskiego Street, and walked towards the front door. The first-floor ice cream shop was empty. Boarded up windows gave the impression the shop had gone out of business but Teddy had witnessed what had happened to its owner and knew it was a completely different story.

He went to reach for the door but before he could grab the handle, someone opened it from the other side.

"Tanchum?" said the woman, astonished at what she was seeing. "Tanchum, is that really you?"

Teddy looked at the woman who knew his name and recognized her as the superintendent of the apartment building. She used to do community service and social work with Touba before the German invasion.

"Have you seen my family?" asked a hopeful Teddy.

"No, not yet, but I'll let you know if I do," said the superintendent.

She hugged Teddy and took a step back to look at him. Her smile told him she was genuinely glad to see him. She then turned and walked down the road, out of sight.

For the next few days, Teddy continued walking around the city, searching for anyone he recognized, but hope dropped lower as each day passed. He went to the center of Lodz where organized lists of everyone returning from camps all over Europe were stored, but it was impossible for him to tell if he knew anyone because he could not remember how to read. Occasionally, people helped, but they were more concerned with finding their own family than his.

After two weeks of searching, Teddy overheard some people talking. They spoke about a place where everyone deported from the ghetto during the *Gehsperre* had been taken and gassed. Even though Teddy had assumed the Nazis murdered his family three years ago, the news was painful to hear. He put his hands in his pockets and stared at the ground as he walked away.

Kwart also lost hope of ever seeing Anna or Rebekah again. Each day, he read the lists and each day yielded the same results. He honored his and Anna's dreams of their future together and opened up his own bakery with the money and jewelry stolen from Görlitz.

It was an immediate success. Teddy worked the streets with bags full of pastries and had no problems selling them all, sneaking a few for himself. Kwart struggled happily to keep up with the demand.

Lodz became a dangerous place for Jews as they resettled. None of the Polish residents wanted them in their city and uprisings began. A survivor tried reclaiming his home, and, after a scuffle broke out, he was murdered. As time went on, more stories circulated about Poles killing Jews.

Teddy enjoyed selling pastries for Kwart but there was nothing else for him in Lodz. Everywhere he went made him think of his family and friends and the memories of his happy past became too painful.

He decided it was time to leave. Teddy said goodbye to Kwart, thanking him for everything he had done for him, and promised to keep in touch. He sold his stolen bicycle, which earned him enough money to make it halfway back to Görlitz.

Teddy boarded the train and studied the conductor's every move. He noted the patterns he walked to punch tickets and the time it took for him to walk through the cabin.

When Teddy's ticket had taken him as far as it could, he put his new knowledge to use. Before it was time for the conductor to enter the cabin and punch tickets, Teddy stepped out and climbed onto the roof of the train to hide. When he got up there he was surprised to see a handful of people with the same idea in mind. On a few occasions, people lost their grip and flew off the train. Teddy had no idea if they survived or not. After he was sure the conductor was out of the cabin, he climbed down, reentered the train and casually walked to his seat.

Görlitz was a completely different place than when Teddy had left it a month earlier. The Russians had divided the city into two halves. One half was German and the other half was Polish. The dividing line between the two areas was the Lusatian Neisse River.

People were no longer free to roam wherever they wanted. In order to cross into the German or Polish part of Görlitz, they needed proper paperwork. The Poles did not want Jews to leave the country, the Germans did not want anyone to enter theirs and the Russians wanted everyone to stay put.

Teddy had no money and no job. He had no idea how to go about even finding work. The Nazis had forced labor on him under penalty of starvation or death. He evaluated his situation and tried figuring out the best thing for him to do to ensure his survival.

He did a few things extremely well. He could sneak around unseen because of his size. He could steal easily if it meant survival. He could bullshit with anyone around him and he spoke Yiddish, German, Polish and Russian fluently.

Walking around the Polish side of Görlitz, Teddy overheard people complaining about the lack of certain supplies needed on either side of the river and how huge delays existed in delivering things across the border.

"Why can't they just deliver the supplies?" a woman complained.

"Damn Russians are making life harder than it needs to be," answered another, consoling the disgruntled woman.

At that moment, Teddy knew how he was going to make his living. He snuck into apartments in the middle of the day after seeing their residents leave for work. He raided their drawers and jewelry boxes and looked under mattresses, which was where most people hid valuables. Before he left, Teddy always checked the basement because that was where people kept what he valued most: food.

With stolen diamonds, gold and money, Teddy was able to buy coffee, which was an extremely rare commodity on the German side. The problem was smuggling it over the border. He could not simply walk into Germany. Teddy did not have the paperwork that permitted him to cross and the Russian guards would confiscate the coffee during inspection. He had to find another way.

He walked along the river, staring at the opposite bank and searching for a way to make his plan possible. And then he found it. A few drainage pipes emptied out into the river. Further down from the checkpoint was an area shallow enough for him to climb. That would be his way in.

The night sky was pitch black with clouds covering anything up that offered the slightest hint of light. Teddy ran down to the river to a dock and commandeered a rowboat. Trying to keep his sound down to a minimum, he carefully lowered the oars into the water and tried his hardest not to splash as he rowed.

Once on the other side, Teddy pulled the boat onto the bank and made his way to the drainage duct. The metal grate blocking the entrance broke off easily from years of rust build-up. Teddy stepped inside, turning to make sure he replaced the cover. The last thing he wanted was for someone to notice the duct was being used for something other than drainage.

The sewers ran underneath all of the German side of Görlitz. Using the sewers, Teddy could have full reign within the city. He picked an exit point and sat down next to it, needing to rest. He shut his eyes and fell asleep for the night.

Teddy's body had been accustomed to getting up before sunrise and he used that to his advantage. While everyone in Görlitz was still asleep, Teddy rose and exited the sewer system. He walked around the German side of the city as if he'd been living there for years. His blond hair and blue eyes never gave anyone pause. Even though he was sixteen years old, the years of malnourishment had stunted his growth and his body still resembled that of a twelve year old. He used the perception of innocence to shield him from people's suspicions.

Teddy walked around town finding out where he could make the most out of his smuggled coffee. He knew he could not simply go up to individuals on the street and ask them if they wanted any coffee. He would surely be caught. Instead, he approached shop owners and inquired with them if they would be interested in buying coffee. The shop owners paid handsomely for it, knowing how valuable it was. They ordered more and asked Teddy what else he could bring. Teddy's answer was always, "You got it."

Before he returned to the Polish side for more coffee, he stopped at a shop and picked up yeast, a rarity in Poland. After the sun had set, Teddy made his way back over the river with the yeast. As the sun rose, Teddy was up making contacts to purchase the yeast and buying more coffee to continue his smuggling operation.

After a few weeks, rumors began to spread about the child smuggler who could deliver anything someone desired. People began telling stories about him as if he was a legend. They described him as "the Ghost of Görlitz". He was a small child who knew the ins and outs of the city. He bribed guards, hitched rides, knew all the hidden routes and was never caught. He looked as though he could be from Russia, Poland or Germany, spoke all of the languages fluently and simply vanished in crowds.

Teddy thought he had found his calling. He had all the money he needed and could buy anything he wanted. There was always a demand that Teddy knew he could supply and he found excitement in completing the task. Occasionally, he looked back at the money he was making and felt guilty about how he obtained it, but it was all he knew how to do.

Back on the Polish side of Görlitz, Teddy sat on a bench admiring the view of the river when a strong hand grabbed his shoulder.

"Are you the Ghost?" a voice asked.

#

22: They Are Freed but Not Free

"Who's asking?" questioned Teddy, keeping his attention on the river in front of him.

"Your reputation precedes you," said the man from behind the bench.

Curious that the man was speaking Yiddish, Teddy turned around to see who he was. The man was much younger than Teddy anticipated, probably early twenties. He was well dressed in civilian clothes, a nice pair of slacks and a blazer, quite unlike the storeowners Teddy was used to dealing with.

"Who are you?" Teddy asked.

"More importantly, are you the man we're looking for?" the man replied.

"Well, that depends on what you need," said Teddy.

"I've been watching you for some time now and know your history. You're a survivor, Ghost, and we can use a man of your talents," said the man.

Intrigued by what he was hearing, Teddy nodded.

"Nobody knows this area like you do, Ghost. You can get around the cities and across the river without complication." The man leaned over and looked Teddy directly in his eyes. "You have an opportunity to help a lot of people," he continued. "If you're interested, meet me here at the same time tomorrow."

He stood up and walked away.

Teddy sat for an hour continuing to look out at the river but his mind was elsewhere. *What did he mean, help many people*? he wondered. The man had definitely captured his attention.

The next day, Teddy sat at the bench and waited for the man to return. Thirty minutes went by but nothing happened. Then Teddy felt a familiar hand touch his shoulder.

"Come with me, Ghost," said the man.

Teddy turned around to confirm who was behind him before standing up from the bench and walking off with him.

"My name is Avi," the man said, introducing himself. "I'm part of a larger organization, the Bricha. As you probably know, many Jews are still at risk in

Poland. It's our job to smuggle these people out of the country and into Displaced Persons Camps in Berlin, where it's safer for them until we can arrange illegal immigration for them to Palestine."

"So where do I fit in?" asked Teddy.

"As I said yesterday, you have an ability to cross the border at will. That's an extremely valuable skill for us," said Avi.

"What will I be paid?" questioned Teddy.

"Nothing," replied Avi. "All of our money goes towards arranging transportation and smuggling refugees."

Teddy looked at Avi, raising a suspicious eyebrow. Why would he want to give up the life he currently lived and the money he was making to work, for free, at a much higher risk to himself?

Teddy turned, facing forward, when something caught his attention. Out of the corner of his eye, he noticed a woman. His mouth dropped open as his eyes widened. He could not believe what he was seeing. The strong resemblance to his mother was too good to be true. She rounded a building and walked out of sight.

"I'll be right back," Teddy told Avi as he ran after her.

When he got to the alleyway, it was empty. Teddy ran down to the end but there was nowhere the woman could have gone. There were no doors or windows anywhere, only a brick wall.

Teddy did not know what to make of what had happened. He was certain he had seen his mother, but she could not have simply vanished into air. Not even the Ghost of Görlitz could accomplish such a feat. Teddy stared at the brick wall in front of him for a few moments, trying to figure things out.

Maybe she's trying to tell me something, Teddy thought as he looked up at the sky.

He turned around and exited the alleyway, heading back to Avi.

"My name is Tanchum, and I'll take the job," said Teddy.

"I hoped you would, Tanchum," smiled Avi.

Avi led Teddy to an apartment overlooking the Lusatian Neisse River. There he met two other operatives for the Bricha: Yosef and Izabella. They were going to cross over the border with Teddy and look after the refugees during transports.

Teddy was surprised to see how organized the operation was. The Bricha had plans laid out for everything; they only needed someone capable of seeing it through.

He immediately went into action. Shortly before the sun rose on Görlitz, Teddy crossed the river and entered the German side. While people were out of their apartments and working during the day, Teddy snuck into a few to steal money and jewelry. As usual, he made his way to the basement for some food before sneaking back out.

Once outside, Teddy walked over to the courthouse where Yosef had explained that he should be able to speak to some men who could get him what he needed. He entered into the large, high-ceilinged foyer adorned with its massive marble pillars and walked up the flight of stairs in front of him. Each step echoed loudly in the expansive room, announcing his presence.

Following Yosef's directions, Teddy eventually made his way to the office he needed and stepped inside. A youngish man, no older than thirty-five, sat behind a desk reading a newspaper.

"I'm told you can help me," said Teddy in German.

"How can I be of assistance?" answered the man.

"I need you to make documents for people to cross the border," stated Teddy.

The man looked at the little boy curiously. He stood up from behind his desk and walked over to Teddy.

"Do you know what you're asking me to do?" said the man. "Why should I risk myself to help you?"

"Because I can make you very happy," Teddy responded.

He reached into his pocket and pulled out a few pieces of gold jewelry and some diamonds he had stolen and presented them to the man.

"And a lot more where that came from," added Teddy.

The man happily obliged and began forging illegal documents for the refugees to pass into Germany.

The hard part was not getting the documents, it was moving refugees across the border. Teddy could easily smuggle up to five people across the river at night and guide them through the sewer system to safety but the need was for far greater numbers than that. He needed to move more than thirty refugees per trip.

In order to do this, Teddy needed to find a way to drive a truck straight over the bridge and onto the German side. The problem lay with the Russian soldiers controlling the bridge.

The following day, Teddy walked onto the bridge and went up to the guards.

"My brothers, my brothers!" Teddy exclaimed in Russian with his hands raised in excitement. "You saved me! I was a prisoner here a few months ago and you rescued me!"

The soldiers did not know what to make of this boy. They lowered down their guard completely when Teddy pulled out a few *mazurkas*. The meringue and almond paste cakes made their mouths water.

Teddy handed a few of them out and introduced himself. He told the guards a few stories about life in the camp before they'd saved him and thanked them. After a few minutes, Teddy said goodbye to the soldiers, got up and walked away.

Two days later, he peered out through the apartment window and saw the same soldiers standing by the checkpoint. He ran down the stairs and out the front door, heading towards the bridge. When he got there, he took out two bottles of vodka, a pack of cigarettes and a few chocolates and handed them over to the guards. After fifteen minutes of casual conversation, Teddy again excused himself and walked away.

After two weeks of showering the guards with gifts and befriending them, Teddy felt comfortable enough to approach them about what he needed.

He informed the guards about the current situation in Poland and how the Jews needed to escape. Teddy promised that gifts and money would come their way if they helped his cause. They agreed. The path was now clear.

In a matter of weeks, Teddy had become one of the Bricha's most ingenious operatives. Hundreds of people were crossing the border every week and making the trek to Berlin.

After two months, a few Russians in charge of controlling the border strongly suspected illegal activity was occurring on their doorstep. According to their documents, too many "Germans" were going from Görlitz to Berlin. They also caught wind that one of the Bricha's head operatives would be making a crossing in the middle of the week. They decided to set a trap.

Teddy pulled up to the border and knew immediately something was not right. The guards he worked with were not staffing the checkpoint. In their place were a few guards he had not seen before. As the truck stopped, three additional guards exited the building to the right of the gate and came over.

"What's your purpose here?" the guard asked.

"Delivering supplies," responded Teddy.

The guard asked for his papers. Teddy obliged but before he could hand them over, the guard pointed his rifle at him and ordered him to get out of the truck.

Teddy cautiously reached down to the door handle, opened the door, and stepped out with his arms up. The two other guards walked to the back of the truck, lifting the gate to see what was inside. At first, it appeared empty but they were not buying it. One guard stepped onto the truck. He searched through boxes and crates and looked under a few benches.

The guards found twenty-four people. Teddy appeared calm and even-keeled on the outside, but inside he was beginning to panic.

"Who's in charge of this convoy?" the guard yelled at Teddy.

"I am," Teddy responded.

The guard's face turned a dark shade of red as he became infuriated with the boy.

"We have reason to expect a lead operative of an organization is on board this truck, and this ten-year-old boy tells me it's him," the guard protested to his comrades.

They laughed, underestimating Teddy's age and ability. The guard grabbed and spun him around to face the truck before asking the question again.

"Who is in charge of this convoy?"

Teddy's answer remained the same, earning him a kick in the pants and an escort to a temporary prison. Two days later, he was moved to a jail in Dresden.

Dresden was a different world. The city had been destroyed during the war. Two buildings could not be found standing next to each other, but, somehow, the jail managed to remain intact.

While in Dresden, the Russian officers began to investigate who Teddy was. Neither the Russians nor Germans believed he was the one in charge of a large refugee operation because he appeared so young.

To make it harder for them, no one even knew where Teddy came from. He spoke fluent Russian to German officers and handed them Russian papers, and he spoke fluent German to Russian officers and gave them German papers.

Finally, after two weeks of dealing with Teddy, still having no answers and viewing him as young and harmless, they decided to let him go. An officer who'd taken a liking to Teddy's fearlessness asked him where he wanted to go, to which Teddy responded "Poland."

The next day, Teddy found himself on a transport back to Görlitz.

When he arrived, a man at the border checkpoint, already paid off by the Bricha, was waiting for him. Recognizing Teddy, he called him over.

"In a little while, I'm going to take everyone here and march them to a building to be screened and registered for prison. When we turn left, go right," the man whispered.

Teddy nodded and walked away.

After an hour of waiting, the man marched the prisoners out of a fenced-in waiting area. Five minutes into the march, Teddy looked up in front of him and saw the prisoners turning left into an old brick building. He did as he was told, and went right, quietly sneaking away.

The Bricha got in contact with Teddy next morning. They decided his services were needed elsewhere and sent a plane for him.

As the wheels glided off the runway, Teddy's face was glued to the window. He could not believe how quickly his life had changed. Just a few months earlier, he was starving to death. Suddenly he was in an airplane, something he never thought possible.

He was flown from Görlitz to Warsaw and finally to Katowice where he met up with one of the head operatives of the Bricha. During their meeting, Teddy found out that they were opening a new point in Szczecin. It would be one of the busiest areas of activity and they had selected him to run the operation. Teddy looked up at the man in disbelief that he was important enough for a role of such magnitude.

"I believe in you, Tanchum. You're the best we've got."

Teddy accepted his orders. The next day he arrived in Szczecin and began making new contacts and putting his team together. Teddy was leery of using trucks; he did not want to chance capture again. Moreover, the sheer numbers of people needing to make illegal passage had grown well into the thousands. Teddy needed to think of something big – and quickly. He decided trains would be the best route.

Things went well for a month. Teddy and his crew had boarded a few cars on the trains. Once aboard, they approached the German citizens heading to Berlin and offered them a deal.

"I'll match the price of your ticket and give you a little extra if you'll allow my friend to take your place," Teddy offered.

Refugees carrying illegal documents for their passage replaced those who accepted. Teddy explained to them the severity and danger of their situation. He educated them on how to act if approached during checkpoints.

"If they speak to you in Russian, you don't understand. If they ask you questions in German, you are Greek. You don't know anything."

The Bricha paid off the conductors and employees of the trains who pretended not to see anything. The real fear lay in the lack of trust with the disembarking passengers but they had no way of knowing illegal activity was occurring. They only knew a person needed to be on board who did not have a ticket.

In that first month, Teddy and his crew successfully smuggled over two thousand people safely into Berlin.

Teddy's reputation grew quickly throughout Szczecin. Eventually, it grew too big. Russian and German guards caught wind of what was happening, found Teddy and his crew, and sent them back to jail. This time around, the guards knew Teddy and were not fooled by his young appearance.

He was placed in a holding cell adjacent to one containing five SS officers who'd been captured while fleeing the country. The jail appeared to be more like a medieval dungeon than a modern prison. The walls were of old stones laid on top of each other. Years of water dripping onto them from a leaky ceiling made them slick with mold. The bars to the cell were old and rusty, and, though it appeared they could easily snap off, were surprisingly strong.

The SS taunted him day and night, making death threats and priding themselves on almost completing the extermination of his people. Teddy was furious. He screamed at the guards for locking him up and treating him the same as SS bastards. They'd murdered his people. He was trying to set them free.

The first week in jail, Teddy tried finding ways to escape. He searched the surrounding areas and pulled at the rusty bars but they would not budge. The more he thought about it, the more it became hopeless.

His second week was more productive as he began plotting new ways to smuggle people. Teddy knew the guards would release him soon and he wanted to have an idea set in place to continue his work immediately. Despite constant torment from the SS soldiers and the hatred growing inside of him towards the guards who had placed him in that cell, Teddy developed a plan.

Two weeks after his capture, Teddy was released. Like the last time, a man working for the Bricha met him at the border, this time escorting him back to a secret location where his team was waiting for him.

Teddy went right back to work. This time he decided to use boats along the Oder River to smuggle people across the border. He befriended and paid off a Russian captain to make the crossings. It was much slower than the trains and greatly decreased the number of people they were able to smuggle, but things went well for three months.

One day, Teddy woke up with a high fever. Each movement he made sent chills throughout his body. He told Micha and Bartek, the two men he was travelling with, that he was not going to make the journey to Berlin.

Micha was a few years older than Teddy. He had lost his entire family in Treblinka and joined the Bricha soon after his liberation. He had a strong desire to be in charge of the transports and was jealous of Teddy always leading the way.

Bartek had earned the nickname 'Lucky' soon after joining the underground. Not because he had extraordinary luck on his side, but because he'd survived the Lodz ghetto and Auschwitz-Birkenau, along with his wife and all four of their children aged from eleven to seventeen. Individuals barely survived. An entire family making it through was unheard of.

Teddy took an immediate liking to Bartek. They had similar pasts, both being from Lodz and surviving Auschwitz, and they took pride in the work they did.

"It's ok, Tanchum, get your rest," said Micha.

"Are you sure?" asked Teddy. "You know the route and the times?"

"We've done this many times before, we'll be fine," answered Micha.

He turned and exited the room, shutting the door behind him.

Teddy rolled over and fell into a deep sleep. He woke up in a cold sweat a few hours later. When he felt strong enough, he got himself out of bed, dressed and walked over to his headquarters.

Walking through the front door, he noticed people were staring at him as if he was a ghost. He didn't think anything of it, given he was so ill and probably looked awful. Teddy headed to Avi's desk and asked how everything was going.

"You didn't hear, Tanchum?" said Avi.

"Hear what?" Teddy answered.

"Micha and Bartek are dead."

Teddy took a step back, trying to digest what he heard.

"What do you mean, they're dead?" asked Teddy. "I only just saw them."

"I'll tell you what I know," responded Avi.

\#

23: Risks and Rewards

Micha and Bartek were going about business as usual. They met up with the refugees at the designated location and explained how everyone needed to conduct him or herself. They had to operate in complete silence. If guards approached them on the opposite side of the river, nobody was to speak. But then the normal routine changed.

Both the Russian boat captain and the vessel were different. The new skipper explained to Bartek that Dmitri, the captain they always used, was sick but that he'd explained his job to him and told him to take over. Not thinking anything of it, and having left Teddy, who was also sick, the two men went along with the mission.

The moon shone clearly in the night sky, casting its reflection in the unusually calm river. Micha whispered to the refugees to quietly board the boat and sit as low as possible. Men, woman and children tiptoed across the wobbly wooden plank and onto the tiny vessel and then found room on the deck to sit.

Finally, Bartek stepped on board, nodding to the captain that everyone was present. The captain slowly pushed off the dock and guided the boat forward into the river. Parents huddled over their children, keeping them warm in the cool night air. One baby began crying but the mother quickly hushed her down with a soft kiss on her cheek.

Halfway through the crossing, the boat engine shut off and it slowly glided to a stop in the water.

"What's the matter?" Micha asked the captain.

"You are," the captain responded.

He reached into his coat pocket, retrieved the pistol he had hidden there and shot Micha in the head. Children began to cry at the sound of the gunshot and their parents screamed at witnessing the murder. Quickly, the captain gained control of the chaos and threatened to shoot anyone who did not listen to him.

"Everyone off the boat," the captain ordered.

"Why are you doing this?" asked Bartek

"To stop the illegal Jew migration," said the captain, with a voice full of hatred. "Now get off the boat."

"But I can't swim," answered a frightened Bartek

"Now's a perfect time to learn," snapped the captain.

He lifted his pistol above his head and fired a second shot.

People scrambled to get off the boat. Mothers held their babies as they jumped into the black river. Fathers struggled to hold their family members' heads above water as they attempted to swim ashore.

Bartek, with no other choice, jumped into the river. He aimed for a piece of luggage floating nearby. As he grabbed a hold of it, the bag began to sink, taking him down with it in a panic. He drowned shortly after.

Teddy stood in silence for a few seconds. He could not get the picture of Bartek out of his mind and he could feel his panic. *His poor family*, he thought. Teddy could not swim either and knew what his fate would have been had he been on the boat. He excused himself from Avi and walked outside for some fresh air.

Thoughts raced through his mind. *Could I have avoided the situation? Could I have stopped the captain? Would the captain have shot me instead of Micha? I should have been on the boat.*

Teddy did not bother going back into the headquarters. He walked back to the apartment, climbed into bed, and cried himself to sleep.

He thought hard over the next few days. The boat operation had worked up until the Micha and Bartek incident but, even at full capacity, it was slow. The most efficient way to smuggle people across the borders was with trucks. Teddy knew it. He'd stayed away from the idea upon opening the northern route of the Bricha for fear of imprisonment, but that trepidation had diminished and it was time to bring the method back.

Over the next two weeks, he worked on his connections to put a plan in place to cross the border with trucks. Teddy and his team had to do most of their driving at night, which meant a great risk to their own lives since they had to drive with their lights off to conceal their passing.

The refugees waited weeks to make the crossing. Most of them were nervous and terrified at the dangers that lay ahead of them. Their lives depended on the success of the trip.

The huddled crowds murmured as Teddy entered into the room. Their expressions changed from ones of confident anxiety to fear. The refugees were all surprised and shocked to see that the leader of the group was a young child who could not be more than twelve years old. Everyone was immediately distrustful of the small blond-haired, blue-eyed boy.

"How could this little boy bring us to safety? He will leave us the instant he hears gunshots!" were common concerns voiced by already-worried refugees.

Members of Teddy's team, noticing the uneasiness throughout the group, did their best to calm them.

"That 'little boy' has brought thousands of people across the border. He is brave and very capable of making the journey," they told them.

The trip through the northern route towards the American Displaced Persons Camps in Berlin was very difficult. The long, hot, cloudless days made refugees wish for cool air and rain. The combined lack of padding on the seats and boxes and the overabundance of bumps on the road made their bodies ache.

The cold rainy nights made them shiver. The sound of raindrops landing on the canvas roof constantly reminded them that they were not yet safe. Teddy looked back into the rear of the truck. Families grouped together, holding one another and using each other's body warmth for heat. He knew what they were going through. Much had happened since then, but Teddy had strong memories of huddling together with his family for warmth during the extreme winters in Lodz.

Teddy admired the people he transported. They were willing to risk everything in search of a better life for their families. The refugees had left most of their lives behind, carrying with them only a suitcase of belongings and the hope that things would be better. As long as the families had each other, they could make it through. Teddy had believed the same when he still had his own family, until the Nazis took them from him. Seeing it again brought back his hope.

As the voyage continued, the children aboard cried in the uncomfortable conditions while their parents showed fatigue, worn down by the long, dangerous trip. It was at these times that Teddy earned their trust.

The truck was two miles away from a checkpoint. Teddy turned around and looked at his frightened passengers. He got out of his seat and walked into the cabin of the truck where he handed candy to each of the smaller children to quiet and keep them calm. He then looked at the older kids, who were not much younger than he was.

"It'll be ok," Teddy said. "Just a minute and it'll be behind us."

Teddy placed everyone in empty crates and hollowed spaces underneath benches to keep them hidden from the guards. He walked back to the front and sat in his seat before turning around to face everyone.

"SHHHH," said Teddy, lifting his index finger and placing it in front of his mouth. He then faced forward as the checkpoint came into view.

The tension grew thick as the truck came to a stop. Many of the refugees held their breath, afraid to make even the slightest sound. Two Russian guards approached, one heading to the driver's window, the other towards Teddy's. They both rolled down their windows, already well aware of the routine.

"What's your business here?" asked a guard.

"Delivering yeast to Berlin," said the driver.

"You want to take over? This stuff smells worse than the Germans!" Teddy joked in Russian.

"How are the roads? Are they clear yet?" asked the driver.

"*Da*, you'll make it through no problem," said one of the guards.

The other guards explained the quickest route to Berlin before waving them through the checkpoint. Once back on the road, everyone breathed a sigh of relief.

"See, no problem," said Teddy, shrugging his shoulders and easing the tension.

Once out of their hiding spots, Teddy joked with the adults to keep their minds off the current conditions and dangers still ahead. He encouraged the older children to take care of each other and the younger ones as well. Knowing the feelings of starvation well and seeing refugees repeatedly not bringing enough food for the long journey, Teddy always packed extra. He saved it for tense moments and handed it out equally to everyone. Food always made everyone happy.

The next checkpoint approached quickly. The refugees were again hidden and their anxiety palpable. The truck stopped in front of the crossbar and waited for the guards to come out.

Teddy turned to the cabin.

"Quiet," he said before facing forward.

Four German soldiers came over. Teddy's heart raced at the sight of their uniforms. It did not matter that the war was over, the attire still terrified him. These people had been responsible for taking away his family and sending him through the depths of hell. His seventeen-year-old mind reduced to that of himself as a ten year old, to the first time he saw those uniforms as they marched on Lodz.

The knock on the window snapped Teddy out of his reverie and sent him into action.

"Sorry, I was dreaming," said Teddy in German, as he rolled down the window.

"Must have been a good dream," answered the soldier. "Where are you heading?"

"Yeast to Berlin," said Teddy, pointing to the back of the truck.

The soldier looked into the cabin through the window, then at Teddy.

"Show me the yeast," said the German.

Teddy's heart picked up again. Usually this checkpoint did not involve inspections. There was always one box filled with yeast in the back that he would open to show anyone who wanted to check the load; the rest concealed people.

Teddy opened his door, stepped out of the truck and led the soldier to the back.

As Teddy opened the gate to the rear of the truck, a refugee sneezed. Keeping his cool and acknowledging the fact that the soldier heard it, Teddy answered the sneeze with "*Gesundheit.*"

"*Dankeschön,*" answered the driver, also playing on the sneeze.

The soldier never caught on. Acting like everything was normal; Teddy opened up a crate and reached in to show the guard a handful of yeast. Two trucks pulled up behind them and honked their horns, waiting to get through the checkpoint.

"OK, you can go," said the soldier.

"Thank you," answered Teddy.

He walked back to the front of the truck and got in. The crossbar lifted and they drove on.

"Who is this boy? Where did he come from? Is he one of us? How can he do those things?" were questions the refugees now asked, having seen what Teddy was truly capable of.

Whenever something needed to be done, Teddy did it. He made himself available everywhere to everyone, all at the same time. He never let on that he was tired or scared but always offered words of encouragement and did everything with a smile.

When the refugees arrived safely at the Displaced Persons Camp, Teddy continued his job to the very end. He made sure everyone received food and shelter and that any other needs were met.

Everyone wanted to thank Teddy and his crew for saving them, but when they turned around, they were nowhere in sight. There was no time for a thank you, only time to rescue more people. They were already on their way back to Szczecin to get ready for the next trip.

The Bricha gave Teddy orders that if a person fell off the truck or was shot, he was to forget about them. Losing one person was better than losing fifty or more.

During his next transport, he was in the first of three trucks making the trip to Berlin. Their precious cargo was seventy children and twenty adults. Teddy had twenty-four children and six adults on his truck. One of the adults caught his eye. She had a strong resemblance to his mother. The way she held her daughter reminded Teddy of how Touba used to hold Esther. As the trip was underway, he spoke Polish to Polish guards at the first checkpoint, Russian to Russian guards at the second and finally German to German guards at the third.

When they came upon the fourth checkpoint, Teddy felt as though he had seen the scenario before. He did not recognize the guard in the booth, nor did he know the sentry operating the wooden crossbar in their way. He knew they had been caught. Thinking fast, Teddy turned around and addressed his group.

"Listen to me. No matter what happens – no screaming, no crying. We'll make it through." He leaned over to the driver and in a single word, gave his order. "Fast."

The driver stepped down hard on the gas pedal sending the truck accelerating towards the crossbar. The burst of speed made a few people lose their balance. The woman who reminded Teddy of Touba yelped as her little girl flew off the truck. His mother's voice echoed in Teddy's head. "Save her!"

Without a second thought, Teddy forgot about his orders and ran through the cabin. He jumped out of the back and grabbed the girl. The other trucks followed orders and continued to drive.

Seeing the vehicles picking up speed and heading straight for him, the guard staffing the crossbar jumped out of the way. A loud crack told Teddy that the trucks had broken through the bar and were speeding off. The guard in the booth pulled out his submachine-gun and began firing it at the trucks.

Hearing noise behind him and seeing Teddy and the little girl running off the road, the guard who operated the crossbar turned and began to fire at them. Dirt began jumping up at Teddy and the little girl as it was displaced by bullets landing at their feet. In one smooth motion, Teddy picked up the girl and ran into the woods. The guards continued to pursue them for half a mile until they finally gave up and headed back to the checkpoint to call in reinforcements.

Teddy and the girl stopped to rest. Teddy tried to listen for anyone who might be approaching them. There was only silence.

"Are you ok?" Teddy asked, looking around the woods to get his bearings.

The little girl nodded but started sobbing as the adrenaline left her system. Teddy reached into his pocket and handed her a few pieces of candy.

"Don't worry, we'll be ok," said Teddy, continuing to be positive and reassure her.

Continuing his mission, even though he had broken a cardinal rule, Teddy began looking for a way to catch up with the caravan. They walked through the forest for a few miles with the hopes of finding a sign of civilization but there was nothing. They carried on walking east when Teddy noticed something that did not look like it belonged in the woods. He grabbed the little girl and hid behind a tree.

Cautiously, he peered around the edge of the tree to get a better look at what he'd glimpsed. It looked like a motorcycle with an attached sidecar. He scoped the area to see if its owner was around but did not see or hear anyone. They left the safety of the tree and headed towards it. The vehicle was an old German military motorcycle and sidecar. Its owner lay beside it, and had been dead for some time. The skeleton was still in uniform and the bullet hole in the skull answered the question of how the man had died.

Teddy helped the little girl into the sidecar then straddled the bike. He reached down and turned the key, hoping for the best. He looked up at the sky and smiled when the engine started with ease. They continued moving east through the forest until finding signs of human life.

Teddy and the little girl hid in an old barn until sunset. Slowly, with the lights off, Teddy rode into the night. He kept the bike off the road, knowing that patrols would be looking for them. He weaved the bike in and out and around trees, slowly gaining ground on the trucks.

Teddy figured that, due to the day's events, the trucks would be taking the emergency route they had outlined before the journey. He was right. As the sun came up the following morning, Teddy saw the caravan. His driver did a double take when he saw Teddy riding alongside of him and stopped the truck. After a quick reunion the trip continued, the little girl's mother thanking Teddy continuously.

On the return trip, Russians stopped the caravan of three trucks. They'd been searching for them for a few days. They pulled the trucks over and inspected them thoroughly, looking in all of the crates and benches, but it was too late.

The soldiers escorted Teddy and his group back to the Polish border where there were people waiting with orders to arrest them. After making the drop off, the Russian soldiers left, not knowing that the Bricha had paid off these people and the prisoners were freed fifteen minutes later.

Teddy ran to the headquarters and phoned the underground head. After telling him what had happened, the head told Teddy to stay out of sight for a few days and that he was sending a plane for him.

Three days later, Teddy arrived in Munich.

People greeted him with applause as he walked into the headquarters. His name was a legend in the underground and Bricha's success was largely due to Teddy's operations. After meeting everyone and shaking their hands, Teddy asked to meet with the head in private.

"I want to go to Palestine," said Teddy.

"There's still a lot of work to be done," answered the head.

"I know, but I've given you a year and have helped many people," Teddy answered. "I have no family, no life of my own. I can smuggle people and steal, but I do not even know what five and five is. I've been in jail repeatedly: it will not end well for me. I want to start over again in Palestine."

"Give me two weeks here in Munich and see if you like it. If not, we'll get you to Palestine," answered the head.

Teddy nodded in agreement.

Over the next two weeks, he did various jobs. He arranged for the transport of hundreds of Jews from various locations, including his home base in Szczecin, to the DPC. He acted as a courier to the underground head and delivered various documents to officials throughout Munich, but, in the end, he still decided his life needed to be in Palestine.

The Bricha arranged for Teddy to be on a special transport. The head offered to have illegal documents forged for Teddy to gain entrance into the country, but he refused them. He'd had enough of smuggling and forged documents in his life and wanted to do this for himself, the right way, even though that meant sneaking himself in illegally.

Teddy boarded the steamer *HaMapil Ha'Almoni* with 806 illegal passengers all leaving France for Palestine. The vessel left in the middle of the night to avoid detection by patrolling British ships aimed at stopping all unlawful entry into Palestine.

The boat was tiny, able to comfortably hold only a tenth of the amount of people currently on board. The conditions brought back memories of the train that had left Lodz for Auschwitz. He had trouble breathing and frequently made his way to the outside perimeter of the ship for air.

The *HaMapil Ha'Almoni* approached Palestine near Jaffo, next to Tel Aviv, after fourteen days at sea. Almost immediately, a plane flew overhead and spotted the ship and all of the illegal immigrants. The captain turned on the loud speaker and told everyone to go inside but it was too late. The British had already spotted them.

In a matter of minutes, four British destroyers surrounded the tiny, overloaded boat. Two of them pulled up next to the *HaMapil Ha'Almoni* and sandwiched it like a harmonica. A small battle began between the destroyers and the people desperate to make it into Palestine.

Before Teddy was able to react, a rubber bullet hit him in the head and he fell to the deck.

#

24: Life Begins At Seventeen

Pain radiated through his body but it did not slow Teddy down. He picked up potatoes and canned goods that were stored aboard and began throwing them at the sailors. People followed suit and began hurling food at the enemy. The British sailors turned on high-pressure fire hoses and began spraying cold water onto the hostile civilians.

The battle lasted an hour and ten minutes until the British finally boarded and subdued the revolt. The *HaMapil Ha'Almoni* was captured by the St. Austell Bay and towed to Haifa by the minesweeper, *Welfare*. Once off the boat, the illegal immigrants boarded a much larger ship, which took them to Cyprus.

When the ship docked in Cyprus and the immigrants began disembarking, Teddy saw his opportunity to escape. Four boys, who worked with the captain as marines, were heading down into the lower levels to work. He noticed that the British were not searching deep into the ship so if he went with them, he would be able to make for Haifa and escape.

Teddy took a further minute to think about it, and then decided to stay with everyone else. He promised himself he would get through whatever lay ahead the honest way and start fresh.

The British directed him to a line and searched him for ammunition and weapons. Once cleared, Teddy walked to another line where everyone had to give up his or her valuables. He had a lot of money and jewelry on him from the smuggling life of his past. The British officers in line took it all away and gave him a receipt.

"Not everything," said Teddy. "I need some jewelry back."

"We need to take everything, sir," said the officer.

"The necklace belonged to my mother and that ring was my father's," Teddy lied.

When no one was looking, the officer handed the jewelry back to Teddy who quickly put it back into his pocket. He had no idea what to expect where they were taking him but he knew he would be better off if he had something of value to trade. He then followed the line in front of him and entered into a camp.

After nine months in the internment camp, the British released Teddy and many other immigrants and gave them legal certificates to enter Palestine.

He arrived into kibbutz Alon, on the border of Lebanon, where they issued him a rifle in preparation to fend off possible attacks from neighboring countries.

The only thing Teddy wanted to do was go back to school. What he had hated the most as a child in Lodz was now all he desired. At the kibbutz, Teddy spent four hours a day working and another four hours learning. In the six months he was there, he tried to catch up on an entire twelve years of education. He learned Hebrew and arithmetic as well as many other subjects.

After six months, Teddy decided that the kibbutz lifestyle was not for him. He yearned for adventure. He left with two other men for Haifa. Life became very hard. There was no work and no money and eventually Teddy went back to his old ways of smuggling.

After a few weeks of this, towards the end of 1949, he decided to join the army and so enlisted for three years. Upon his deactivation from the military, an officer who knew Teddy's past involvement in the underground asked him what he planned on doing.

"I don't know what to do," Teddy responded. "I'm only good at smuggling and driving trucks."

The officer knew someone in a nationwide bus company named Egged. He told Teddy it would not be easy but he would try to get him in for an interview.

Two days later, Teddy went in to meet with the president of the company. Initially, the president did not think much of the twenty-three year old but was blown away after hearing his stories and driving experience with the Bricha. He hired Teddy on the spot.

In the beginning, he had to prove his dedication to the company. They put Teddy on the nightshift. To an average person, the hours were horrible, but to Teddy, who had done most of his work with the Bricha at night and was used to surviving on almost no sleep while in the concentration camps, the hours were not that bad.

He arrived for work at 4am and sometimes 3:30. At the headquarters of the company, he picked up a list of bus driver addresses. From there, he picked up a bus and drove it to a station to have it cleaned and filled with gas. He then drove around and picked up the drivers and transported them to their buses.

Life came together for Teddy. Two months into working for Egged, he had proven his commitment as a worker. He underwent a complete physical and background check and was made a full member of the company. In Egged, a member held the same amount of shares as the president and held a strong and positive status in the community.

In June 1955, Teddy was walking around town with one of his friends from the company. The two ordered falafels from a street vendor. When his friend reached into his wallet to pull out money, four pictures fell to the ground. Teddy noticed a photo of a family.

"Who's that?" asked Teddy inquisitively.

"Who, this?" the friend responded, pointing to the picture.

"Yeah," Teddy answered. "Is it your sister?"

"No, she's not my sister!" the friend laughed. "That's my neighbor's daughter, Rivka."

"Do you think I can meet her?" asked Teddy.

"You can, but I don't think she'll even look at you!" the friend joked.

"Why not!" Teddy asked playfully.

"She is looking for a tall man with curly hair who likes dancing. You're none of those!" his friend laughed.

Teddy insisted that he had to meet the girl in the picture. He could not explain it, but he felt a strong connection to her. His friend arranged a meeting between the two of them a week later.

At 5pm, Teddy nervously walked up to the door of Rivka's apartment. He had survived unspeakable things and his life had been on the line more times than he could remember, but nothing made him more nervous than that moment.

He reached up with a sweaty hand and knocked on the door three times, then took a step back and waited. After what seemed like an eternity, Teddy heard the bolt unlock and the hinges let out a quiet squeak as the door opened.

Rivka was standing there with her mother, Pola. Teddy's eyes went into tunnel vision as his heart pounded, making him lightheaded. He reminded himself that everything was ok, took a deep breath and introduced himself to both Rivka and her mom.

Not knowing Teddy spoke Russian, Pola turned to Rivka and, in their native tongue, told her that the boy looked strangely familiar to her. Rivka did not know what her mother was talking about. She told her mom she would be right back and walked out of sight. Five minutes later, she returned, and the two of them went out on their date.

Teddy took Rivka out to dinner and then to a place where they could dance. He had no idea how to dance and figured he was making a fool out of himself, but as long as he could impress her, he was doing all right.

The two of them danced and until one in the morning. He learned that she was seventeen and originally from Odessa, Russia. Her father was in the army and had been killed in an early battle with Germany. Her family fled the country when the situation worsened for them there. Her five brothers and sisters all perished on their journey. Rivka was now a student in school and learning how to speak English. Her mother, Pola, had remarried after they moved to Israel.

"Can I take you out again tomorrow?" Teddy asked, on the walk home.

"No," replied Rivka bluntly.

"Why not?" Teddy questioned, feeling the wind leaving his sail.

"I have school tomorrow," answered Rivka.

"After school?" asked Teddy.

"I can't," responded Rivka.

For every day that Teddy mentioned, Rivka had a story as to why she could not see him. Finally, after going through two weeks of Rivka's schedule, Teddy said enough was enough.

"I'm picking you up at school next Thursday. We'll tell your mother and we'll go out somewhere."

Impressed by his persistence, Rivka agreed.

Two weeks later, Teddy picked her up at school and the two of them walked over to her apartment.

"*Privet, kak dela,*" said Teddy to Pola as she opened the front door.

Taken aback by the young man greeting her in Russian, she smiled and let them into the apartment. From that moment on, Teddy developed a close relationship with Rivka and her parents. They loved him and everything about him. Teddy had not felt love like that since losing his parents thirteen years earlier. He knew this was where he belonged.

Over the next few months, Rivka's family learned many things about Teddy. He was shy and did not speak much, especially about himself, but always listened and helped others. He had no family – the Nazis had killed everyone he loved during the war – but he was not angry or spiteful. He had learned from his past and used it to build his future. He was confident in his ability to survive and he proved it repeatedly. His love had no boundaries and everyone around him loved him equally as much.

In November of 1955, three months after they started dating, Teddy and Rivka were married in Tel Aviv. A few weeks later, Rivka and Teddy were eating dinner at her parent's apartment. An hour of casual conversation went by when the topic of how Rivka's family migrated to Israel came up.

Pola knew Teddy was involved with the Bricha but he had never gone into detail about how deep his involvement lay. She began to talk about their journey to the DPC in Berlin. How they'd met at a secret location in Szczecin and waited a week for their rescuers to arrive. Pola explained how scared they were when a little blond-haired, blue-eyed boy, no older than twelve or so, arrived. They thought he was a German or Russian *goyim* who would turn on them the first chance he had.

She then mentioned how the little boy had gone above and beyond for them to make them feel safe. How he took care of the younger children and entertained the adults, making the terrifying conditions bearable. How this boy seemed to know every language in the world and spoke them with minimal effort. All of the soldiers he spoke to at the checkpoints knew him and let him through without problem.

Pola than began to talk about one checkpoint that had put the boy at unease. He did not recognize the soldiers standing guard. She explained how the boy told the Russian driver to drive fast enough to break through the crossbar, but as the truck jolted forward in its acceleration, her daughter Rivka...

"Fell out of the back of the truck," Teddy interrupted.

Pola stared at Teddy trying to figure out how he could know that. It was not until she looked into his blue eyes that she understood.

"It was you."

#

25: Life

"You mean, Saba rescued Baba?" asked Hayden.

"That's right, Hayden," I said, looking at her through the rearview mirror. "And they didn't even know it until that moment."

"Wow, that's crazy," said Shannon, joining in on the conversation. "It had to have been meant to be. Look at how happy they are."

"I want to hear more about Baba and Saba!" stated Hayden, excitedly.

"That's a story for another day. We're almost here," I answered.

Once over the Tappan Zee Bridge, the sun broke through the clouds. The traffic mysteriously dissolved after passing the Palisades Mall. It was as though everyone on I-87N had taken the exit to see one of the largest malls in the country. Now, almost to Baba and Saba's house, it appeared no rain fell at all. I searched the road for puddles, telling myself I was not imagining the torrential downpour we'd experienced on the way over, but there were none in sight.

Hayden and Shannon continued asking me questions about Saba's childhood for the remainder of the drive. Their interest in his life told me that I had at least done a decent job telling the story.

"Finally!" I shouted, putting the right blinker on and pulling into the driveway.

Cars were parked everywhere and it was evident that we were the last ones to arrive. Almost everyone at the party came from around Rockland County. A few people had driven from Brooklyn or New Jersey, but they had not hit the heavy traffic from Connecticut.

"At least it's not a surprise party," joked Shannon, as she opened up the car door and stepped outside.

The rain had definitely not fallen anywhere near the house. The cars were completely dry. The music coming from the back yard also told me people were enjoying the party outside.

"Hayden!" shouted Eti, appeared from around the corner.

"Hi Grandma," answered Hayden, as she hurried towards her grandmother. "Dad told me Saba's story."

"Oh, did he?" said Eti, giving her granddaughter a hug.

"Yeah, he did. I didn't know he went through all of that," said Hayden.

"Saba has had quite a life, that's for sure," answered Eti.

She walked over, giving me and Shannon a kiss, then led us to the back of the house.

"Traffic was bad, huh?" asked Eti.

"Oh yes," I answered. "You have no idea."

The backyard was full of people. In one corner, people danced to the twist. In another, a few individuals waited in line for the barbeque. My dad, Bob, was running the grill while keeping people entertained with his sense of humor.

"Hayden!" a voice shouted over the noisy crowd of people.

"Aunt Gab!" yelled Hayden, as my younger sister Gabrielle walked over to see her niece.

Looking around the party, I knew almost everyone there. My older sister and brother, Aimee and Bobby, were talking to a few people in the kitchen. Aunt Tova and Uncle Michael, whose cement platform I'd been helping Saba pour when I learned of his past, were sitting at a table eating with my cousins, Seth, Emily and Paige.

A couple of Saba's reunited cousins were also standing around talking.

#

In the early 1990s, Rivka and Teddy were at the Miami Holocaust Memorial Museum when Rivka came upon something interesting. When looking on the list of over 300,000 people from Lodz, she found a few names listed together:

Szajna Touba Minski

Esther Minski

Tanchum Lajb Minski

Teddy's last name was Znamirowski. He'd always looked for Znamirowski when searching for family but never thought to look under his mother's maiden name.

Rivka knew everything about Teddy's past. What made these names interesting was not only that they were listed together, but the possibility it could actually be Teddy's mother, sister and Teddy himself.

Teddy had escaped from the holding area at the hospital in Lodz undetected. To the Germans, Teddy was just a name on a list. Having been selected for deportation during the *Gehsperre*, it was assumed he'd been sent to Chelmno and gassed with his mother and sister.

Rivka was determined to find out who'd supplied the names to the Holocaust Museum. After a lot of back and forth, she was able to get a name out of them. It was Bronia Rosenfarb.

Teddy immediately recognized the name. She was a second cousin on his mother's side. Rivka wasted no time in contacting her. The screaming on both sides of the phone was deafening as the second cousins heard each other's voices for the first time in over fifty years.

Bronia was in touch with other relatives who'd survived the war, over forty of them. She contacted them immediately and told them the news of Tanchum. With one phone call, Teddy went from having no family members from before the war to having many of them.

She also mentioned a woman named Rose who lived in New Jersey, only thirty minutes from Teddy. *Could it be*? Teddy thought to himself.

Two days later, Teddy and Rivka drove down to Jersey to meet this Rose. She was very old and had a lot of trouble moving around but Teddy knew exactly who she was. It was his Chuh Chuh Rose, his beautiful aunt, whom he'd spent most of his childhood with, the mother of Cila.

From then on, family – old and new – always surrounded Teddy.

#

"Come Hayden, let's go say happy birthday to Saba," said Shannon.

Shannon, Hayden and I slowly made our way to Saba, stopping constantly to say hello to someone. Everyone needed to tell Hayden how big she was and wanted to fill his or her pinching cheeks quota for the day, despite her being well over "pinching cheeks age".

A red-faced Hayden finally made it to Saba. He sat back comfortably on an Adirondack chair next to one of his best friends, Gabai, who had also emigrated to the US from Israel. The two of them laughed and joked in Yiddish while eating grilled chicken and an Israeli salad.

Hayden's whole perspective of Saba had changed. He was always a kind, loving man to everyone, and especially his great-granddaughter, but now, knowing his past, she had developed a deep respect for him.

"Hi Saba!" said an enthusiastic Hayden.

"Hello, my beautiful girl," answered Teddy.

"Happy birthday," said Hayden with a big smirk.

"Sank you, beautiful face," said Teddy, returning the smile.

Hayden leaned in to give her Saba a hug and a kiss and whispered in his ear, "Saba, why do you talk like that?"

Teddy pulled back and looked at his great granddaughter. Clearing his throat, he started, "Growing up wasn't easy for your Sa."

Hayden put her finger up to his mouth, cutting him off.

"I already know," said Hayden, answering her own question.

Saba gazed upon his great granddaughter, understanding what she had said, then leaned back in and gave her a tight hug. He looked up at me as I stood there smiling, watching my daughter and grandfather embrace.

As we made eye contact, Teddy shed a tear and nodded in appreciation. His biggest desire in life was for people to know what he had been through so they could stop it before it happened again. Now another generation knew.

Continuing to hug Hayden, Saba motioned with his hand for me to come closer. I leaned in and hugged my grandfather.

"My beautiful boy, I love you," said Teddy.

"I love you too, Saba."

The End

About the Author

Erik LeMoullec is a chiropractor and acupuncturist residing in Southbury, Connecticut, with his wife Shannon and their two daughters, Hayden and Reese. He received his B.S. Degree from Oneonta State University in 2004 and his Doctor of Chiropractic degree at the University of Bridgeport in 2008.

Growing up a first-generation American in a Jewish household in Monsey, New York, was interesting – a strong emphasis on family heritage and a layer of Jewish guilt covered everything. After listening to the horrific and heroic episodes of his grandfather's youth, Erik believed they were for a greater audience. Together with his grandmother, he observed as Teddy lectured audiences at middle/high schools, Holocaust museums and libraries, resulting in inquisitive questions and disbelief. When taking over the reins and presenting his grandfather's story himself, the results continued.

To book clubs and groups of ten members or more:

Erik will address, in person, any gathering within a thirty-mile radius of Southbury, Connecticut, or within the New York metropolitan area. He will address gatherings outside of those areas through Skype. Erik can be contacted at eriklemoullec@gmail.com or through his website backtohealthwoodbury.com Follow him on Twitter @DrErikLeMoullec